Battered Bride?

By the same author:

Truth in the Son
Believing the Bible
The Search for the Real Jesus
Walking in the Light
    (Confessions of St Augustine)

BATTERED BRIDE?

THE BODY OF FAITH
IN
AN AGE OF DOUBT

David Winter

MONARCH

Eastbourne

Biblical quotations are from the New International Version
© International Bible Society 1973, 1978, 1984

Jacket design by Peggy and Drummond Chapman

British Library Cataloguing in Publication Data

Winter, David, *1929–*
  Battered bride? : the body of faith in an
age of doubt.
  1. Great Britain. Christian church, to
1980s
  I. Title
274.1

ISBN 1–85424–000–5

Printed in Great Britain for
MONARCH PUBLICATIONS LTD
Lottbridge Drove, Eastbourne, E Sussex BN23 6NT by
Richard Clay Ltd, Bungay, Suffolk.
Typeset by Nuprint Ltd, Harpenden, Herts AL5 4SE

The church's one foundation
Is Jesus Christ, her Lord;
She is His new creation
by water and the word:
From heav'n He came and sought her
To be His holy bride,
With His own blood He bought her,
And for her life He died.

Elect from ev'ry nation,
Yet one o'er all the earth,
Her charter of salvation
One Lord, one faith, one birth;
One holy name she blesses,
Partakes one holy food,
And to one hope she presses
With ev'ry grace endued.

Though with a scornful wonder
Men see her sore oppressed,
By schisms rent asunder,
By heresies distressed,
Yet saints their watch are keeping,
Their cry goes up, 'How long?'
And soon the night of weeping
Shall be the morn of song.

'Mid toil, and tribulation,
And tumult of her war,
She waits the consummation
Of peace for evermore;
Till with the vision glorious
Her longing eyes are blest,
And the great church victorious
Shall be the church at rest.

Yet she on earth hath union
With God the Three in One,
And mystic sweet communion
With those whose rest is won:
O happy ones and holy!
Lord give us grace that we,
Like them, the meek and lowly,
On high may dwell with Thee.

Samuel John Stone (1839–1900)

ACKNOWLEDGEMENTS

In the preparation of this book I have been deeply indebted to a number of people. All of the statistics quoted, unless otherwise indicated, are based on Peter Brierley's work in and for the *UK Christian Handbook* 1987/88 edition, published by MARC Europe. In addition, Sarah-Jane Elbourne has contributed enormously to the arrangement of the material and the preparation of the manuscript, and Philip Winter carried through the practical organisation and processing of the survey of the Anglican clergy.

CONTENTS

CHAPTER ONE

THE AUTHOR'S
HEALTH WARNING

THE BIGGEST DANGER ABOUT THIS BOOK is
that both the author and his readers will take it too
seriously: a fault not unknown in religious circles. I
have set out to offer one man's view of the life of
the Christian Church in Britain today, not a magisterial survey
of the world of religion. It will be partial, incomplete, preju-
diced and at times (doubtless) factually incorrect. It is not a
work of reference or an encyclopaedia of religion: indeed, I
have tried to keep footnotes and references to a minimum.
The author would claim to be reasonably well informed, but
not infallible. The book is sure to make its readers grit their
teeth at times. I can only hope that their justifiable annoyance
will be largely offset by the entertaining spectacle of a person
in my position making a fool of himself.

However, there seem to be good reasons for taking that
risk. The chief one is that there is an enormous amount of
interest in the Church today, but much of it is ill-informed.
With half the population *never* crossing the threshold of a
church, and another quarter only doing so once or twice a
year, that is hardly surprising. I hope that those readers at
present outside the committed membership of the Christian
Churches will find this an entertaining and informative
glimpse into what goes on within those doors week in and
week out. They may be surprised—or even shocked—to
learn how things have changed over the last couple of decades.
What is certain is that much criticism (of the 'boring-sermons-
empty-pews-mumbo-jumbo' kind) is as out of date as the

church life it tries to depict. If people decide to stay away from church, well and good: that is their right. But let the reasons for doing so relate to the Churches as they are, not as people in their forties remember them from their childhood.

The second reason for writing the book is to give Christians an overview of the Church as a whole. Almost all of us are, at heart, parochial. When we say 'the Church' we mean the one *we* attend (or choose to stay away from). Few of us are in a position to know whether the broad and sweeping generalisations made by press and prelates are true or false. Is the Church in crisis? Are congregations still shrinking? Do bishops doubt the faith? Most of us can only scratch our heads and wonder.

However, nearly thirty years of covering religious news, seventeen of them in religious broadcasting, have given me an almost unique opportunity to see across the usual parochial fences. I have been in churches of every denomination, from Roman Catholic to House Church, from United Reformed to Seventh Day Adventist, from Baptist to Brethren. I have met the leaders of most denominations and many other groups, including the great non-Christian faiths. Perhaps more significantly, I have been on the receiving end of literally tens of thousands of letters and have had access to the BBC's in-depth audience research to remind me that the Church does not exist for its leaders, but for its members . . . and those who are not yet its members. As I have said, I am not infallible. Indeed, when you turn to a chapter on the area of Christianity which you know best I think I can guarantee that you will disagree with it. But what I lack in depth I make up for in breadth. Never mind the quality; feel the width.

For the Churches of Britain represent a bewildering kaleidoscope of ideas, images, impressions and beliefs. They are involved not only in the worship of God (under a hundred different rituals), but in education, politics, history, philosophy, ethics and the arts. If this book is in essence a series of personal sketches, then they embrace a vast panorama of human experience. Not all of it will appeal to every reader, and truth compels me to say that not all of it appeals to me. But it is all part of the rich tapestry woven by the beliefs and experiences of seven million diverse believers.

Because this *is* one man's view—a series of personal

sketches—it is essential that the reader should learn to allow for my particular bias. It is all very well to say, as I do, that I have tried to be fair. One person's fairness is another one's prejudice. So the reader should know that I am an Anglican, an 'open' evangelical, an ordained clergyman in my fifties. I know southern England well and west Wales fairly well. For the rest I am a visitor and observer, and much of what I know is essentially second-hand. I am not charismatic in theology, though I would claim to be open to the gifts of the Spirit. I am unable to accept some elements of traditional Roman Catholic doctrine, but have learned to appreciate catholic spirituality beyond any other. I have ministered widely in Free Churches over the years and was once (many years ago) offered the pastorate of a Baptist church. Now I am anxious that all these Churches should press towards the goal of visible unity in the holy, catholic Church. I know several of the House Church leaders very well and have many friends—and indeed relatives—in the movement, but I cannot disguise my anxiety about schismatic tendencies, however and wherever they surface.

Yet, in contradiction of my prejudices, I really do believe that *in all things*, as St Paul says, God works for the good of those who love him (Rom 8:28); and 'all things' includes our party spirit, our sectarian tendencies, our carping and criticism of the way others respond to the universal grace of God. Even in the writing of this book I have found my spirit warmed by the recognition of God at work in every part of his Son's divided body—the battered Bride of Christ. I hope and pray that it will not fuel or promote strife, but will instead promote the love that he sheds abroad in our hearts—the love that witnesses to the truth that all who love the Saviour are inescapably and eternally one.

CHAPTER TWO

DREAMS AND NIGHTMARES

I SAT IN THE LEADING CHOIRBOY'S SEAT and surveyed the congregation scattered haphazardly around the pitchpine pews. The sermon moved inexorably on. The sunlight explored the worn patches in the red chancel carpet. The choir numbered twenty-seven; the congregation twenty-two.

I can remember the figures to this day, though I cannot exactly place the Sunday. It was probably the early summer of 1945, just before my voice broke. It was the beginning of the post-war period, with plenty of bomb-sites in our North London suburb, and street and park air-raid shelters lending themselves to pursuits for which they were never intended. It was the era of ration books and coupons, of *ITMA* and *Much Binding in the Marsh* on the radio, of the Labour landslide in the General Election. Slowly the men were coming back from the war, including my older brother. But they never came back to church. According to the statistics, it was the beginning of the end of mass church attendance in Britain. Certainly the figures tell us that church attendance then was overall a great deal higher than now—probably double what it is today, over forty years later—but was about to fall dramatically.

Yet to me, as a teenager growing up in the Church, and as a pretty active church member over the whole of the subsequent forty years, those were the wasteland years of the Church. The war—like the Great War twenty-five years earlier—had disturbed many traditional patterns of life and had challenged many hitherto unquestioned assumptions. It is true that people packed into the churches for the National Days of Prayer called by the king; it is the only time I can remember seeing the place literally overflowing. But for many the cruel reality of war, and the sheer struggle for survival after it, relegated churchgoing to a minor place in their priorities. Not only that, but the Churches seemed largely irrelevant to all the most important things going on around us. The world was changing: anyone could see that—anyone, that is, except the majority of those who led the Christian Churches. For them, it was a return to the old formalities— the *Book of Common Prayer*, or the echoing chapel with its equally antiquarian 'hymn sandwich'—that Britain really needed.

Britain may have needed it, but what Britain wanted, as it emerged from the long, dark tunnel of World War II, was *change*. That was the message of the first post-war election, when the 'old men' who had led Britain into it, and through it, were rejected for a fresh set of faces, many of them largely unknown to the general public.

There were prophetic voices in the Churches, it is true, among them the outstanding wartime Archbishop of Canterbury, William Temple. They could see that change was inevitable, in the Church as well as in society in general. So did many an army chaplain, returning to parish life with a whole new understanding of how 'ordinary' people felt about Christianity. But they were isolated voices.

My abiding memory of churchgoing in that period is of a deadly formality, of empty pews and incomprehensible services. Perhaps in some church—a few miles away—there was enthusiasm, commitment, colour, excitement. But if there was, I knew nothing of it. If that really was the closing act of the great age of British churchgoing, I must have arrived just after the curtain came down.

Today, according to those statistics, many fewer people go to church. The Church, we are told, cuts little ice in the life of our society. Christian ministers are unsure of their role and their message; lay people are outnumbered, beleaguered and bewildered. An inevitable and apparently irreversible process of decline has set in, which has seen the total figures for

church attendance and membership fall in every successive
year for four decades. So we are told.

Yet the Church I observe today, as an ordinary member,
as a minister, and as a religious journalist who has covered
church affairs professionally since 1959, is manifestly more
alive, more committed, more effective, more relevant and has
a higher public profile than ever before in my lifetime. My
own church—not three miles away from the one where I was
a choirboy—is hardly packed to the doors, but the services
are vigorous, colourful and relevant; the members are enthusiastic, well-informed and loyal; and its impact on the district
(a typically multiracial London suburb) is considerable . . .
and it is the same in that church of my childhood.

In the course of my work I visit scores of churches every
year, of all denominations and in every part of the United
Kingdom. I can honestly say that there are many more like
my own present church than there are like the dull ecclesiastical relic of my childhood. Whatever the figures say—and
as I shall explain later, I think their message may be
misleading—the Churches of Britain look to me to be in
remarkably good heart.

Not only that, but the public at large is aware of them in
a new way. When I joined the BBC in 1970, there was no
religious affairs correspondent, simply because there was very
little religious news. For the same reason there was no
religious news magazine on the radio, and no regular religious
documentary series on television. How different it looks
today, with religion often front-page news in our papers, with
the BBC's religious affairs correspondent a household name,
and both radio and television giving enormous prominence
to religious news and ideas, and attracting large audiences for
them.

There is obviously a fascinating paradox here. Church
attendance *has* gone down. Church membership *has* declined.
Fewer people say they believe in God. Yet interest in the
Church's message—that is to say, in Christianity and its
founder, Jesus Christ—seems to be higher than ever. And
people who do not belong, who choose not to belong, nevertheless look to the Churches for a lead in all manner of moral,
ethical and spiritual issues. Whatever Britain is today, it is
not a 'secular' society, in the sense that it has no regard for

spiritual values. It may have forgotten the way to church, but it has not lost its soul.

I have begun this book in this rather personal, autobiographical style because that seems to me to be the only effective way of approaching a daunting task. I have set myself to look at the Churches of Britain in these final years of the twentieth century, to try to see how they have got where they are, and to ask where they might go next and how they will get there. To do that it is obviously necessary to sift and record a great deal of evidence, and much of that evidence is, of course, statistical.

But it has never been, and is not now, possible to report spiritual activity solely in these terms. Counting heads does not tell even half the story. After all, Jesus changed the course of human history with twelve apostles and a couple of hundred disciples, one of whom was a traitor, some of whom were unreliable and ineffective, but most of whom were fired with an other-worldly sense of commitment. I shall have to look at structures, at bishops and synods and reports and organisations, and they will reveal this and that about the way the religious life of Britain has changed and developed. But to know what has really happened we have to try to enter into the heart of the life of the Christian Church—yes, and into the hearts of ordinary Christians.

For in the end what will survive will not be buildings or organisations, but an idea that has fired the hearts of men and women for two millenia. It is the extraordinary power of the Christian gospel not only to change lives, but also to build a living community that is at the heart of church history, and it is, I believe, the explanation of the paradox that runs right through this book. The Church can survive and flourish when the outward organisation is in decline. Indeed, it usually does. The first sign of a renewal in the Church is seldom people enrolling for church membership, but a rise in the spiritual temperature outside, in the 'world'.

This I believe is what we are beginning to see—a dissatisfaction with material, secular answers, and a deep, though argumentative longing for those very values that the gospel of Jesus has always represented: the awareness that we are loved by our Creator, that we can be accepted, forgiven and remade, that every single human being is valuable because

made in God's image, and that no one is beyond the scope
of his redemption. The more technology flourishes and the
more impersonal the business of our daily lives becomes, the
more precious is the vision of another kind of society, one
where righteousness dwells and God's will is done. It is the
work of the Church to nourish that vision, not to count the
number of its adherents.

So I do not believe that we are today witnessing the terminal
decline of the Christian Churches in Britain, but that is not
to say that I do not accept that they face massive problems.
The tide of faith may be on the turn (rather than on the ebb,
as Don Cupitt suggested in his *Sea of Faith* series on television), but that does not automatically guarantee a
flourishing future for the Churches. There are now other
outlets for religious experience, other ports where the fragile
craft of the spiritual seeker may find a welcome.

The dream may be of a nation rediscovering its soul, and
turning again to the faith of our fathers. The nightmare could
be of a society which finds its deepest questions unanswered,
its unvoiced longings unmet by the Churches—and turns,
instead, either to hedonistic materialism or irrational superstition. There are precedents, for both the dream and the
nightmare. The decisive factor may well be the willingness of
Christians to face the challenge, and the sometimes painful
changes that it may demand of them.

CHAPTER THREE

HOW WE GOT TO WHERE WE ARE

I T SEEMS A FAR CRY FROM THE WANDERING PROPHET of Nazareth to the secretariat of Church House, Westminster. Borrowed boats on Galilee and word-processors flickering out statistics of clergy training do not seem to have much in common. Yet the Churches of Britain, in all their diversity, share one absolute conviction: that their starting point and origin is Jesus. They are *Christian* Churches, and owe their existence to the appearance on the stage of world history of that charismatic preacher, healer and prophet who came to be revered as Messiah and Son of God.

But it is not only a long trek from Galilee, where it all began, to Canterbury, Edinburgh and Armagh. It is also a complex one. The processes of church history through the intervening two thousand years have crucially affected the way the Churches are today. They may all claim a common allegiance to Jesus Christ. They may also each claim to represent the faith in its purest, most original and biblical form. But there is not a single Christian denomination or group in Britain that has not been influenced, and even shaped, by something that has happened in that long corridor from first-century Palestine to twentieth-century Western Europe.

EARLY DAYS

The Romans brought Christianity to Britain in the second century. It took root and spread across the islands. The first British martyr, Alban, died in about AD 303 in one of the periodic bouts of persecution that marked the Church's existence during the dying centuries of the Roman Empire. But by the fifth century the faith was under pressure from another source, as the Angles (in the north and east) and the Saxons (in the south) swarmed across the country, bringing with them their Teutonic gods and driving the Christian Britons into the hills of Wales and Scotland.

Here, however, it flourished. Celtic Christianity, as it is known, was to become a major force in the later re-evangelising of Western Europe. It was a faith of intense personal devotion, nourished in the monastic life of prayer and self-denial, and increasingly distinct from the Roman Church, which was painfully trying to adjust to the changing world of the new Europe. Bishops and princes struggled (often literally) for supremacy in the former Roman Empire of Western Europe; while in Ireland, Wales and the Western Isles of Scotland a fresh and renewed kind of Christianity was quietly establishing itself. St Patrick (385–461) was the first great figure of this movement, evangelising Ireland and then building a missionary movement based on a string of monasteries that carried the gospel to every corner of the Celtic world. We can see the next phase of that movement in men like St Columba and St David in the sixth century, who almost certainly had their roots in the Irish Church but spent their lives evangelising and church-building in Scotland and Wales.

Meanwhile the re-evangelising of England had begun. In 597 Pope Gregory I sent Augustine across the English Channel. King Ethelbert of Kent was converted, and over the following century much of what is now England accepted the faith.

This meant, of course, that there were now two 'versions' of Christianity in the British Isles: the Celtic version, with its origins in Ireland and its monasteries and priests scattered across Cornwall, Wales, Scotland and much of northern England; and the Roman version, based on Canterbury and covering most of southern, central and eastern England. The bishops of the two jurisdictions met at the newly founded Abbey of Whitby, in North Yorkshire, in 664—the Synod of Whitby. The Celtic Church, for historical and geographical reasons, had had little contact with Rome, though it recognised the special place of the Bishop of Rome in Christendom, and its leaders were anxious to avoid any threat of schism. Some may feel they were too anxious, for the eventual agreement, a truly historical event, conceded almost everything to the Roman bishops. However, unity was achieved, and perhaps as a consequence the British Church, nourished by the strengths of two powerful but distinct traditions, was the major influence in Western Europe for several centuries. One of its monks, Boniface, was the leading figure in the evangelising of what we would now call West Germany and the Lowlands in the eighth century. 'Boniface' does not sound a very English name, of course. But his original name, 'Winfrid', denotes his origins in Anglo-Saxon society.

That period of great spiritual power and influence for the British Church, epitomised by such figures as Cuthbert, Boniface and Bede, perhaps helped to establish the independence of the Church in these islands. Although Canterbury was loyal to Rome, it was never as slavish in its devotion as some of the great sees of Southern Europe, nor was its relationship to the Pope as tempestuous. Those twenty-odd miles of sea have had a great deal of influence on the ecclesiastical as well as the political history of Britain.

THE MEDIEVAL PERIOD

Still, the Channel was crossed, on the best-known date in British history, 1066, when the Normans conquered the southern kingdoms and William planted not only French customs and language but also many continental clergy in his new realm. The English language was never the same again, of course, but neither was the English Church. It was not only architecture that changed, as massive Romanesque cathedrals—Durham, for example—began to tower over the English landscape. For a few centuries the English Church was more thoroughly integrated with its counterparts on mainland

Europe than ever before or since. It was a period of relative calm in the Church before the storm that was to break in the fifteenth and sixteenth centuries. Not that it was without strife. The princes and the Pope squabbled over jurisdiction—for nearly seventy years Avignon, in Provence, was the Papal see, while various parties strove to establish their candidate as Pope—and the abuse of power in the Church became a public scandal. The low esteem in which ordinary people held the monks and clergy can be seen from some of the figures in Chaucer's *Canterbury Tales*. It was not surprising that in various parts of the continent reform movements began to surface in the fourteenth century. The first and most influential of these began in England, under the leadership of John Wycliffe (1328–84).

Wycliffe denied the Church's authority in temporal affairs, which had been the most contentious issue throughout the Middle Ages. He held Scripture, not the Pope, to be the supreme authority in the Church, and preached against the doctrines of transubstantiation, penance and priestly absolution. He made the first translation of the Bible into English, and his followers, called Lollards, carried his message throughout the land and beyond. Because he had some degree of support from powerful men—notably John of Gaunt—he managed to die of natural causes. Although condemned as a heretic (which, by contemporary standards, he certainly was) he was never sentenced. John Hus, in Czechoslovakia, followed Wycliffe's ideas but lacked the loyal support of influential people and was executed in 1415—an event that led to the Hussite Wars. There had been a minor rebellion in England the year before as a protest against the persecution of the Lollards, but their influence had waned by the time of the Reformation controversies a century later.

THE REFORMATION

Wycliffe and Hus were undoubtedly precursors of the Reformation. Both were motivated by anger and disgust at the corruption and decadence of the medieval Church. The Renaissance, with its opening of windows to new knowledge, created a fresh environment, as did the invention of printing.

But the pressure for change came from below as well as from the intellectuals, and much of the support for Wycliffe and Hus was from ordinary peasants and the newly emerging merchant class, who were aware of abuses and impatient for reform.

With Martin Luther (1483–1546) this sense of impatience found an intellectual and theological focus. An Augustinian monk, Luther probably intended no more than to call the Church to reform itself. Certainly he was very reluctant to encourage schism. His rediscovery from St Paul and St Augustine of Hippo (both, after all, deeply revered figures in the medieval Church) of the doctrine of grace led him to his distinctive theological innovation, the phrase 'justification by faith alone'. By this he meant that the 'sinner'—that is, fallen human personality—is justified before God not for any good works he may perform, but solely and utterly on the basis of his faith in Jesus Christ.

Luther's views would not have sounded strange or particularly innovative to Augustine. That very concept, almost in those words, can be found in the *Confessions*. But it did sound strange to a Church which had developed over the period of the High Middle Ages an incredibly complicated system of rewards and penalties, of sins, penances, indulgences and purgatory, depending very largely on the doctrine of merit. To them, Luther's ideas sounded anarchic. Was he really saying (he was not, of course) that you could sin away to your heart's content so long as you had faith in Christ? Was he alleging that the merits of the saints were of no value in our salvation, or that what we did—in alms, in gifts, in purchasing indulgences—was so much vapour in terms of standing before God?

It was a dialogue of the deaf, for the most part, and the split, when it came, was the predictable mix of theology and politics, with a few princely old scores being paid off while the former Augustinian monk protested that all he ever wished to do was convince Pope and Church that St Paul and St Augustine were right and that the medieval Church had taken a wrong turning and needed to retrace its steps back to the truths of Scripture.

Luther, and his more iconoclastic counterpart in Geneva, Calvin, did have their supporters in other parts of Europe. In

Britain their ideas fell, as we have seen, on prepared ground. William Tyndale (1494–1536), a disciple of Luther's, published an English translation of the New Testament in 1526. This was at once denounced, and copies were seized by the authorities; but it is harder to confiscate an idea. Tyndale himself was executed in Antwerp for heresy ten years later, but by then Henry VIII, enraged by what he saw as papal interference in his somewhat bizarre matrimonial arrangements, had declared himself Supreme Head of the Church of England and initiated a break from Rome that provided the hitherto cautious English Reformers with a chance to influence events.

The Archbishop of Canterbury at the time of the break with Rome was Thomas Cranmer. He it was who annulled Henry's marriage to Catherine of Aragon despite the Pope's specific orders to the contrary. Trying to assess motives long after the event is difficult, if not futile, but Cranmer subsequently revealed strong Reformation tendencies, which suggests he may not have been altogether dismayed by the break with Rome. He encouraged the translation of the Bible into English—this within a year or two of Tyndale's execution for doing precisely that—and under Henry's successor, Edward VI, compiled in two stages the Prayer Book which was to shape the worship and doctrine of the Church of England for the next four hundred years. It was a further century before the Act of Uniformity (1662) made that book (in substance—it was another revised version) the only, exclusive and official liturgy of the English Church. In the interim there had been a brief resurgence of Roman Catholicism under Mary I when Cranmer himself was burned at the stake, and a rather longer period of Puritan rule in the 1650s under the Lord Protector, Oliver Cromwell.

The Puritan period serves as a reminder that not all the British reformers were happy to find their home in what many saw as the merely partly reformed Church of England and its counterparts in Ireland, Wales and Scotland. Many Calvinists preferred a Presbyterian system, free from what they saw as a monarchical, unbiblical episcopacy. John Knox, the great Scottish reformer, succeeded in establishing Presbyterianism as the national form of Christianity in Scotland after the abdication of Mary Queen of Scots in 1567. Others were even more radical, notably those dubbed 'Anabaptists', who opposed the baptism of infants and, even more riskily, preached the total separation of Church and State. Throughout the sixteenth century they were persecuted all over Europe. Indeed, the first English Baptist congregation was formed in Amsterdam, early in the seventeenth century, under John Smyth.

Another element in British Christianity after the Reformation was Congregationalism. A dynamic preacher, Robert Browne (1550–1633), led a group of dissenters, inevitably dubbed 'Brownites', who believed in the independence and autonomy of the local congregation (unlike the Presbyterians), and were consequently totally opposed to the idea of an established Church. Browne's ideas deeply influenced many of the early settlers in America, but it was not until the closing years of the seventeenth century that the Toleration Act gave any legal status to such dissenting groups in England and Wales.

At the same time as the Protestants (as they were known) were painfully aligning themselves into the groupings we now know as Anglicans, Presbyterians, Congregationalists and Baptists, the Roman Catholic Church was engaged in the Counter-Reformation, or the Catholic Reformation. This was an attempt, culminating in the Council of Trent (1545), to deal with admitted abuses in the Church, and also to counter the new doctrines of Protestantism by restating the dogmas which had been most ferociously besieged during the sixteenth century, notably those connected with justification, transubstantiation and eucharistic sacrifice.

THE EVANGELICAL AWAKENING

As the eighteenth century began, the pattern of Christianity in Britain—Anglicans, Dissenters and a brave Roman Catholic remnant—was to suffer a further major disruption with the Methodist, or evangelical, revival. Probably in reaction against religious extremism epitomised by the wars and heresy-hunting of the previous centuries, British Christianity in the early eighteenth century had become calmly, not to say coldly, rationalistic. Religious enthusiasm was seen as a danger to public order and a sign of emotional immaturity. Much of the Church of England's life, in particular, was formal and nominal; and many of the bishops and clergy were more occupied with hunting, socialising or acquiring plural livings than with providing pastoral care for the ones they already had. The Church had a Reformation liturgy, but at heart it remained stubbornly unreformed. At the same time, it lacked the mystical streak that had been a redeeming feature even of the darkest days of the medieval Church.

A strong pietist movement on the Continent, which had made considerable headway in the Lutheran Church, began to attract attention in Britain, particularly from clergy dissatisfied with the nominal, worldly and careless state of the Church of England. Two brothers, John and Charles Wesley, both Anglican clergymen, were among them. John was disillusioned with his ministry and returned from a visit to America in 1735 desperate to find the kind of evangelical fervour he had seen among the Moravians. These spiritual descendants of John Hus had been greatly influenced by the pietist movement, and preached the need for a personal conversion to Christ. John Wesley experienced this while listening to a reading of Martin Luther's commentary on Romans in London in 1738. He felt his heart 'strangely warmed' and discovered that he did trust Christ, 'and Christ alone', for his salvation.

With the support of his brother Charles, who found a similar conviction, and of an eloquent preacher (George Whitefield, from whom the Wesleys eventually split over the issue of predestination and free will), John Wesley spearheaded a national mission to bring this evangelical message to every part of the British Isles. Since most church pulpits were closed to him, he preached largely in the open air, and he was spectacularly successful, as was Whitefield. Like Luther before him, John Wesley had no intention of creating a schism, but the formation of classes for converts, the establishing of a network of methodist groups (again it was the nickname that stuck: they were so methodical in their spirituality) and finally the ordaining of clergy for methodist missions in the colonies, all made the split inevitable. Charles lived and died an Anglican, but John saw the beginnings of the Methodist Church before his death. Indeed, the separation from the Church of England and the end of his own life occurred in the same year: 1791.

But many Methodists, or Evangelicals as they preferred to be called, stayed in the Church of England and its sister churches in Ireland and Wales. By the early nineteenth century they were a large and influential group in the Church, controlling powerful bodies like the Church Missionary Society, and also exerting considerable influence in society at large. With a few peaks and troughs, evangelicalism has been a considerable influence in the Church of England right to the present day—indeed, latterly it has been more evident in the Anglican than in the Methodist Church, where a more liberal theology has generally predominated in the twentieth century.

The nineteenth century was a period of great religious activity in Britain. The repeal of the iniquitous Test Act in 1828—an Act which required all holders of civil and military office to take the Oath of Supremacy, declare themselves against transubstantiation, and receive Communion under the Anglican rite—removed many social and public barriers against Roman Catholics and some nonconformists. The following year's Catholic Emancipation Act completed the process and paved the way for the establishment of a Roman Catholic diocesan episcopate in Britain in 1850. Since that time the Roman Catholic Church has grown rapidly, largely through immigration from Ireland, and has become an accepted part of national life.

The nineteenth century also saw the birth of the Brethren movement, the Plymouth Brethren as they were dubbed. This was begun by a Church of Ireland clergyman, J N Darby, and by a group of men, mostly in the West Country, who wished—like many before them—to rediscover the simplicity and purity of the early Church. One may charitably pass over whether even the Church of the Acts of the Apostles was all that 'simple' or 'pure'. What one cannot pass over is the inevitable tendency of purist movements to split . . . in the interests of purity, of course. So the mainstream of the Brethren movement remained at heart a broad and open-hearted body, while various groups broke away from it over this issue and that, some of them surviving to this day as closed Brethren of one kind or another. The Brethren were matched by a number of other revivalist movements—among

them the Catholic Apostolic Church of Edward Irving, probably the first charismatic adventist group to make a mark in
Britain; and the Seventh Day Adventists, coming to these
shores from America in the 1860s.

THE CATHOLIC REACTION AND AFTER

Of more lasting influence than these revivalist groups was the
Oxford or Tractarian movement, launched in 1833 by an
Anglican clergyman, John Henry Newman, with a famous
sermon in Oxford and the start of a series of *Tracts for the
Times* (hence the nickname 'tractarian'). This was the birth
of the Anglo-Catholic movement in the Anglican Church. It
began as a counterblast to theological liberalism and State
infringement in church affairs. But it became a movement to
recall the Church of England to its role as the catholic Church
of this land, committed to the doctrine and ministry of the
undivided Church and distinguishing carefully between catholicism and *Roman* Catholicism.

The distinction was somewhat blurred when Newman and
several of his associates—Ward, Faber, Manning—left the
Church of England in order to join the Roman Catholic
Church. At first the Tractarian party was in turmoil; but
under the leadership of Edward Pusey, it regrouped and began
the slow task of winning over a substantial number of clergy
and lay people to an essentially catholic view of the Church,
while remaining loyal Anglicans. The reverberations of this
exercise continued throughout the Victorian era, with the
ritualists (as they were called by their opponents) being taken
to court, and even committed to prison, for attempting to
bring back into the Church of England such alien ornaments
as crosses, candles and altar frontals, or such attire as stoles,
albs and chasubles.

A glance at the Church of England today will demonstrate
the degree of their success where the outward appearance
of worship is concerned. Whether the Anglo-Catholics have
managed to win the hearts of many lay people, especially, to
a catholic theology or spirituality is more open to question.
As the Church of England remains stubbornly unreformed,
so it remains equally stubbornly non-catholic. Probably J H

Newman's description of it (in his pre-Roman days) as a *via media*—a 'middle way' between Roman Catholicism and full-blown Protestantism—remains the truest evaluation.

Towards the end of the nineteenth century, when the Christian Churches were recovering their breath after a brief and rather pointless battle over Charles Darwin's *Origin of Species* (1859), two new and significant movements began, both of them born in the working-class areas of the big cities. The Salvation Army grew out of William Booth's concern for the spiritual and practical needs of ordinary men and women, particularly in London's East End. It was given its name in 1878 and became a powerful force during the last decades of the century.

Then, very early in the twentieth century, the modern charismatic movement made its first appearance (if one excludes the Irvingites) in Britain. A prayer meeting in a parish church hall in Monkwearmouth, near Sunderland, became the scene of manifestations of tongues (*glossolalia*), prophecy and healing. Subsequently the movement progressed for the most part outside the established Churches—until, of course, the 1960s, when what had been called pentecostalism became known as the charismatic movement, and began to infiltrate all the historic Churches.

. . . AND NOW

That, in a brief, over-simplified and perhaps slightly romanticised summary, brings the history of Christianity in Britain up to the present day. One can see in this century several new, or re-emergent, emphases. Certainly the ecumenical movement, whose origins are generally seen in the Edinburgh Conference of 1910, has made headway, though it has achieved little in terms of actual church unions. The various parts of the Methodist Church—Primitive, Wesleyan, Calvinistic and so on—did come together in the 1920s; and more recently, in 1972, the United Reformed Church brought together English Presbyterians and Congregationalists. But, despite two serious attempts, the Anglicans and Methodists have failed to unite, and most ecumenical effort is now put into attempts to encourage all the Churches to work and worship together as far as possible in a local setting, as we shall see later.

While the Churches were spending much time and emotional energy on attempted moves towards unity, other groups of Christians were opting out of the church scene altogether. From small beginnings in the 1970s, the restoration movement (also referred to loosely as the House Church movement) grew rapidly in the 1980s. Without involving vast numbers the House Churches, like the Brethren in the previous century, provided an alternative model of Christian fellowship from that offered by most mainstream churches, one which particularly appealed to disgruntled or disillusioned church members. We shall look at this movement in more detail later, but its influence—noisy, confident, charismatic—has been out of all proportion to the size of its membership.

The House Churches are charismatic, for the most part, but there are undoubtedly many times more charismatic Christians in the mainstream Churches. In England they are to be found mostly in Anglican and Baptist Churches, in Scotland and Wales in independent evangelical Churches, and in Ireland in the Roman Catholic Church. But all over the United Kingdom the picture is much the same—most congregations of any size, and of virtually any denomination, will have at least a handful of worshippers who are charismatic in theology and practice. And even those who reject the theology have been subliminally influenced by the practice: worship in all the Churches is markedly less formal than it was twenty years ago. The charismatic songs and hymns, too, have made their way into the repertoire of many Churches where charismatic theology is still regarded with suspicion.

Worship is also beginning to be influenced by another major new grouping of Christians, those in Black-led Churches. After the waves of immigration from the Caribbean in the 1960s many black Christians found it difficult to settle in the established Churches. Partly this was a matter of style— even the Caribbean Anglicans were used to a more whole-hearted kind of worship, and those from the Free Churches felt inhibited by the British convention of congregational immobility and silence. Sadly, part of the problem was the inability or unwillingness of white Christians to accept and welcome black members. Soon uniquely Caribbean Churches began to open in urban areas and attracted many who had never really settled into the British way of worship. They also began to win the allegiance of some who had formerly belonged, often only nominally, to one of the 'old' Churches. These new Churches were mostly charismatic in style (though not always in doctrine) and often had a strong adventist element, reflecting the religion of the slaves, which was the soil from which they had grown. The Church of God of Prophecy and the New Testament Church of God were soon to become the largest and most active Churches in many neighbourhoods—and by the 1980s were producing much vibrant, exciting choral music, increasingly attracting a multi-racial congregation. Many white youngsters found their approach more attractive than the rather more cautious style of the local parish church.

Despite all these new influences and developments, the Churches of Britain are still manifestly children of their parents. A tough streak of independent thinking persists. There is still a good deal of suspicion of prelacy. Puritanism is seldom far below the surface, as the campaign to reject the Sunday Trading Bill in 1986 demonstrated. Above all, however, there is still a widespread respect for the Bible, and an often unspoken dislike of ritual—the latter a strange trait among the people who gave the world the Trooping of the Colour, the State Opening of Parliament and Test cricket.

The great groupings of churches remain: the Roman Catholics, of course, with their emphasis on historical continuity; the Anglicans, holding in tension (uneasily at times) that catholic continuity, the theology of the Reformation, and the more liberal approach of much modern Protestantism; the Presbyterians, heirs of Calvin and Knox, struggling to reinterpret their tradition in the modern world; and the Independents, mostly Baptist in theology, congregational in church order and, nowadays, often charismatic in worship. In modern Britain there is a good deal of friendly rivalry, of course, but also much practical co-operation between these groups. The British Council of Churches has channelled much of this but has been greatly weakened by the unwillingness in the past of the Roman Catholics to become more than observers, and by the strong suspicion of some evangelical groups that the Council is doctrinally vague Obviously the proposals for a new ecumenical association including the Roman Catholic Church, represent an important development, though some Evangelicals might dislike it. But the truth is that only some such body can get within touching distance of all the denominations. Locally and nationally, it is the Council of Churches or nothing, to be realistic. Most churches do belong at least to their local council, even if unenthusiastically, and co-operate on events like Christian Aid Week.

But the differences stubbornly refuse to go away. And perhaps it is best that they remain, as landmarks of the Church's pilgrimage from apostolic times to the present, rather than disappear in some half-hearted compromise. Church membership, measured by the number of people who actually go to services, has undoubtedly declined, but there is little evidence that the differences between the denominations have greatly contributed to that decline. After all, churchgoing in the UK is highest in Northern Ireland, where the differences are at their sharpest. Strong beliefs, strongly held, are the most obvious characteristic of growing churches, now as in the past.

The Churches of Britain have a rich heritage. The prayers of the Celtic Church, the dignity of the Roman Church, the independent thinking of the Lollards and the Reformers, the dogged courage of so many dissenters—Baptists, Congregationalists, Roman Catholics—the simple, personal faith of the early Methodists and the splendid vision of a renewed catholicism of the Oxford movement: no Church in Christendom is planted in more fertile soil. Even the apparently struggling Church of today cannot pretend that it is not the child of its parents, and that rich mixture of loyalty, spirituality, courage and dogged, even stubborn independence, still shapes its life, its worship and its witness. It is much too soon to write the obituary of a Church like that.

CHAPTER FOUR

THE CHURCH IN THE EIGHTIES

A SERIES OF VIVID IMAGES AND SOUNDS, like a cinematic montage, flashes through my mind when I try to create a mental picture of the British Church in the 1980s. I see the Pope and the Archbishop praying together in Canterbury Cathedral; I watch Terry Waite walking away from his protectors and the press photographers in Beirut, his shoulders set, his mission impossible; I hear Bishop David Jenkins, his voice choking with emotion, pleading to synod for the freedom to dissent from the historic teaching of the Church; I remember Billy Graham at Sunderland, the wind blowing icy rain into his face, inviting his freezing audience to repent and believe; the glowing faces of the families at Spring Harvest and the youngsters at Greenbelt; the wave of exuberant sound washing over me from the young black men and women who make up the London Community Gospel Choir.

There are other, less pleasing, memories as well: angry men in clerical collars shouting the obscure slogans of Ulster politics on our television screens; arid disputes over liturgy, the ordination of women and the appointment of bishops—culminating, on one bleak occasion, in the suicide of a distinguished Anglican don; MPs accusing Christian ministers of dabbling in politics when they try to address themselves to such issues as urban poverty or racial intolerance; and the haunting picture, like a sombre backdrop to the whole, of city-centre churches, walls daubed with graffiti, doors and windows boarded up, mute reminders of a past age of faith.

The trouble with memories is that that is all they are: pictures and sounds that have impressed themselves on the screen of our memory, for whatever inexplicable reason. The *impression* I have is of an age of religious controversy and change. It takes a determined effort to remind myself that most eras of church history have been marked by controversy and change, and the exceptions were generally periods of decline. In the 1980s religion was news in Britain, to a far greater extent than in the preceding decades, and religious believers of one kind or another were conspicuous in society. It is worth reminding ourselves that people like Terry Waite, Mother Teresa, Cliff Richard, Desmond Tutu, David Jenkins, Billy Graham and Victoria Gillick—names that have seldom been out of the news for long—are all well-known as Christians, whatever their other qualifications. And the list could be extended to include many more well-known people in politics, law, commerce, sport and the media. Christianity has not had a higher profile for half a century at least, even if the pews are slow to fill up.

The main Churches in Britain have been preoccupied with four things during the eighties: social relevance, renewal in worship, mission and (rather less urgently, one feels) unity.

THE CHURCH AND THE POOR

Undoubtedly the alienation of many working-class people from the Church, especially in the run-down areas of the big cities, seemed to accelerate during the 1960s and 1970s, and this made many church leaders re-examine their pastoral strategy. But as soon as they did this, they realised that the gulf was not simply a matter of culture, language or style. The Church was not seen to be addressing itself to the questions being raised by our new society—questions related to work, technology, housing, apparent or real social injustices and, of course, racial tension. Jesus had good news for the poor. Where is his message for the new-style poor of the late twentieth century?

Of course, since the beginning of the Industrial Revolution Christian voices have been raised on behalf of the exploited and oppressed in Britain's cities. But the new awareness is that philanthropy, even sacrificial loving service, is not enough. David Sheppard, the Bishop of Liverpool, in his book *Bias to the Poor*, argued that the Church should recognise God's preferential concern for the poor and helpless, and align itself unashamedly with the powerless sections of British society. He was hardly the first to say this. Six hundred years ago John Ball led the Peasants' Revolt with the slogan, 'When Adam delved and Eve span, who was then the gentleman?' Both the Evangelicals and the Oxford movement in the nineteenth century bred a streak of radical concern for the poor, and from the centre ground of English Christianity Charles Gore and William Temple more recently raised their voices for social justice.

But David Sheppard represents a new emphasis. In many ways he and those like him are the public voice of the inarticulate and the unchurched. London's East End shaped Sheppard's thinking, when he was Warden of the Mayflower Family Centre. Until then he was a typically earnest, slightly 'plummy', public school and Oxbridge evangelical curate, serving his title at that historic strong-hold of evangelicalism, St Mary's, Islington. He played cricket rather well, and captained England. But that would not cut much ice in Canning Town, where a couple of goals for West Ham would have been a better passport to fame.

David Sheppard took over one of the old dockland settlements, classic examples of Victorian philanthropy and places where tough young men were coached in muscular virtues and taught the optimistic manly Christianity so beloved of World War I chaplains. He realised that approach could never succeed in the East End of the 1960s. The 'settlement' was renamed the Mayflower Family Centre, and its emphasis changed. It stopped trying to turn working-class lads into middle-class ones, and instead set out to help all age groups and both sexes to make the most of their lives in the new urban wasteland of East London. Part of that help—as it had been in the latter years of the old dockland settlement—was to introduce people to the Christian gospel. But it went far beyond that. Old people, young mothers, young men and women and children were catered for. David Sheppard and his team, all of whom actually lived in Canning Town, painfully learnt that identification generally precedes successful service. Most of them, including their leader, felt they learnt more than they taught. The traditional pattern—contact, conversion, removal to a more congenial habitat—began to be challenged. But it is hard to tell a newly-converted young couple, who are now thoroughly disenchanted with the life-style they have known all their lives, that they should stay where they are and try to help others like themselves. In the inner city, housing, education, health care and personal security are all demonstrably inferior when compared with the suburbs a few miles away. Those who stay can be trapped in a cycle of deprivation.

It was this realisation that made David Sheppard decide that something more than evangelism was needed. The whole way we organise our society—its priorities, preferences and standards—had to be challenged. No amount of phil-anthropy, and no amount of individual evangelism, could hope to change things in the radical way that was needed.

So the evangelical curate became the episcopal social reformer. Canning Town began the process. Woolwich (where he was area bishop) continued it. Liverpool, with one of the country's highest rates of unemployment, confirmed the message. Over a period of ten or fifteen years David Sheppard came to accept much of what many others, of a totally different theological background, had been saying for many years. *Bias to the Poor* goes much further than his earlier *Built as a City*, and includes thinking from the Liber-ation Theologians, and a good deal of the anger with which Anglo-Catholics like Kenneth Leech attacked entrenched social conservatism in the Church. Leech, in fact, stands in a long if intermittent line of inner-city priests who since the time of Queen Victoria have allied themselves with their suffering flocks. In that respect they were also like William Booth, whose book *In Darkest England* opened some eyes to the appalling physical, social and moral squalor of the East End of a century ago. Booth, however, did not challenge the basis on which society was constructed. He wanted something done about poverty, but he did not want the structures of society destroyed. He believed that things could be reformed within the system. Leech and Sheppard, from hard experience, have come to believe that something more radical is required, and although they do not go nearly as far as the Liberation Theo-

logians in Latin America, they and those like them in the
Jubilee Group, the Urban Theology Unit and the Evangelical
Coalition for Urban Mission, want something more than
gradual improvement. They want the whole balance of power
and wealth to be moved away from the haves (who have
'never had it so good') to the have-nots (who have seldom
had it worse, at any rate in the twentieth century).

Such ideas have an attraction for many Christians,
especially those concerned about the continuing and perhaps
growing alienation of the urban poor from the Church. In
England it is doubtful if industrial workers have ever been
very enthusiastic about church membership, though surveys
in the middle of the nineteenth century did find quite high
levels of churchgoing even in artisan areas of big cities.
Certainly the Church of England has for long had a middle-
class image. Its clergy are still predominantly middle-class—
many of them public-school educated—and its appeal, as a
literate, 'reasonable' Church, is mainly to literate, 'reasonable'
men and women. Both the Roman Catholics and the freer
Free Churches (such as the mission halls and the Pentecostalists) have had more success in the urban ghettoes: colour,
symbolism and raw emotion have offered more to the residents of these concrete and brick deserts than well-argued
sermons and the *New Cathedral Psalter*.

So a collective guilt consciousness (perhaps)—together with
an awareness that if the drift were to continue the Church of
England and the main English Free Churches would disappear
from the inner cities entirely—has created a climate in which
the social relevance of the Church has become a high priority.
In synod people kept saying that something must be done.
The something eventually emerged as a report by the Archbishop of Canterbury's Commission on Urban Priority areas,
rather more memorably entitled *Faith in the City*.[1]

The publication of the report, in November 1985, itself
largely the work of social scientists and clergy from inner-city
areas, was something of an ecclesiastical *cause célèbre*. In its
way it was a microcosm of the media's general treatment of
religious issues, and evidence of the sensitivity of politicians
to criticism from religious sources. The report was, in fact,

[1] *Faith in the City* (Church House Publishing, 1985).

embargoed until the late evening before the day of its release, a Tuesday. The press office at Church House was especially careful: a previous report, *The Church and the Bomb*, had been unhelpfully leaked and attacked in the press before synod members, for whom it was ostensibly intended, had even had a chance to read it. So *Faith in the City* was carefully restricted. Only serious specialist journalists were allowed to see it a couple of days in advance. Indeed, many journalists and broadcasters were irritated at the curtain of secrecy that was spread over the document.

They were even more irritated when leaks, obviously based on the text itself, appeared in the weekend papers, together with scathing comments from some leading Conservative politicians. One described it as Marxist, which it was not; others regarded it as a typically simplistic piece of priestly meddling in political matters. Most assumed that it was a direct challenge by the Church of England to the elected government of the day: a call to the nation's political leaders to change direction (to make what the press call a 'U-turn') and reverse its fundamental policies of enterprise, competition and self-help.

The criticisms were, in substance, extremely unconvincing. The report was not much concerned with political questions, and not at all with allocating blame. It was not simplistic in its analysis of the problem, almost all of which was based on government statistics and eye-witness evidence, though some of the proposed solutions do have a touch of Utopia about them. It was not a challenge to the government, but to the whole of society, and *especially* the Church; more than half of the report was directed to the leadership of the Church of England. And it did not question the need to create wealth by enterprise and competition. It simply asked questions about the distribution of the wealth and resources so created.

It was, in any case, not the voice of the Church of England, but a report in the name of a handful of individuals invited by the Archbishop of Canterbury. That report would only become the 'voice of the Church' when and if General Synod, the Church's parliament, were to endorse it. In the case of the earlier report, *The Church and the Bomb*, the view of the majority of those submitting it was categorically rejected by synod—though many politicians seem not to have noticed.

A group dynamic builds up within committees; without it, one wonders if any report would ever get written. But the sponsoring body is not bound by the fruit of that dynamic. It may—synod almost always does—receive such a report. But only full debate and a majority vote makes a report into official policy. The unilateralism of the bomb report never became Church policy. Much of the *Faith in the City* report did—especially those recommendations which fell within the competence of synod to fulfil. But few synod members saw that as a challenge to the government—except to try harder. Even fewer saw it as the springboard of a social revolution: synod, as we shall see, is not in the business of revolution.

CHURCH AND STATE

The media reaction to *Faith in the City*, as to the Church's allegedly independent stand over the Falklands thanksgiving service four years earlier, was prompted by a journalistic stereotype of the Church of England rather than by the facts. The press and most broadcasters really believed that the Church was part of the Establishment, the 'Tory party at prayer'. For many of them, this stereotype was based on their own experiences in public-school chapels—for many senior people in the media their only or most recent experience of the Church. They accepted the caricature of sherry-sipping bishops, bomb-blessing chaplains and fluting-voiced curates because they had little first-hand experience of the Church as it is now. In fact most clergy do not vote Conservative. Few bishops are addicted to sherry. It is probably forty years since a chaplain blessed a bomber. And while it would be untrue to say there are no longer *any* fluting-voiced curates, most of the younger clergy, men and women, are fairly robust characters, not much concerned about impressing the local squire and his lady.

But it is hard to dispel deep-rooted illusions. The bishops are appointed by a system that involves the Prime Minister and the Queen. The senior bishops sit in the House of Lords. Bishops and other clergy appear on great State occasions—coronations, funerals, royal weddings—and take their place among the great and good of the nation. These are the

building blocks of the stereotype. But in fact the Church of
England has steadily distanced itself from 'the establishment'
for many years. Most of its leading figures would describe it
as having a prophetic role in the nation—and prophets are
traditionally awkward, disturbing, argumentative people.
Certainly few active church members would tolerate the
Church of England's accepting the role of State chaplain,
simply giving a religious gloss to the nation's great events.

So it was not the regular churchgoers who were surprised
by the tone of *Faith in the City*, just as they were not surprised
that the Dean of St Paul's did not want the trappings of
military triumph paraded in his cathedral at the Falklands
service. What they *were* surprised at was the media reaction
and, perhaps, the way some politicians rose to the bait. The
Faith in the City controversy was almost entirely artificial. It
bore little relevance to the actual contents of the report, as
those who had bothered to read it realised. The row over
the Falklands service was in much the same category—a
misapprehension turned into a media spectacular. There was
no dispute of any consequence between Downing Street and
the cathedral chapter, and none of any description at all
between Downing Street and the Archbishop of Canterbury.
I have it from those most closely involved that the Prime
Minister professed herself 'very happy', with the service. So
much for newspaper talk of a 'furious' Mrs Thatcher, and of
snubs for Dr Runcie. The truth is that the Church failed to
satisfy the media's stereotype of its role; and so, in a totally
predictable reaction, parts of the popular press decided that
it had been taken over by 'pinkoes' and pacifists.

Actually the Church of England is struggling to evolve a
new model of establishment, perhaps more like the Scottish
one. After all, no one expects the Church of Scotland to toe
the Government's line, or meekly acquiesce in policies which
it considers morally wrong or bad for Scotland. The Kirk's
Church and Nation committee has a long history of cocking
a snook at government policies—Labour ones, as well as
Conservative. But few commentators conclude from that that
the establishment north of the border is crumbling. This may
be because the settlement in Scotland gave much more independence to the Church. One can imagine the reactions of
Scotsmen if the prime minister of the day claimed any rights

in the appointment of a new moderator, or the minister of St Giles' Cathedral.

These issues about the relationship of Church and State do not only concern the two formally established Churches of the United Kingdom. To a greater or lesser extent, all of the mainstream churches have adopted a higher profile in recent years on matters of social and political concern. Even the most distinctively evangelical groups—the more conservative Baptists, the inter-denominational Evangelical Alliance and the Free Evangelical Churches—have begun to involve themselves in socio-political matters. They tasted a kind of victory over Sunday trading, where these groups were in the forefront of the fight. But they have also involved themselves in disputes over such things as abortion, euthanasia, censorship, the obscenity laws, education, broadcasting reform and Russian dissidents. Sometimes they have found themselves opposing the government. Sometimes the enemy is a left-wing council. Either way, the distinction between Church and State—one of the great foundation principles of the Independent Churches—is becoming blurred. Perhaps some Christians have taken note of the impact of religious pressure groups in other countries, notably Poland and the United States, and simply cannot resist the temptation to do likewise.

However, probably a more accurate explanation is a theological one. I have said that British church leaders did not, for the most part, accept wholeheartedly the ideas of Liberation Theology. But they were profoundly influenced by its example. This movement really came to prominence in 1980 with the assassination of Archbishop Romero of El Salvador, shot dead in his cathedral while celebrating Mass. He had just read the Gospel: 'Unless an ear of wheat falls to the ground and dies, it remains alone. But if it dies, it produces much fruit.' So it has transpired. The latent anger of many priests at the social injustices around them, at the hopelessness and despair of the poor, boiled over into calls for action rather than talk. They popularised a newly minted word from a Greek root, *praxis*—crudely, 'action'. They argued that it was time to obey the gospel, and that was a call not to discuss but to do, not to watch hopelessly but to change things. Their favourite biblical model was Moses and the Exodus: God becoming involved in direct, and if necessary violent action to liberate his oppressed people. The leading liberation theologian, Gustavo Gutierrez, argues that Christ is our Moses, the liberator who offers an inclusive salvation, one that takes in the whole of reality—not just the soul or spirit, but society itself.

This theology of the kingdom, as distinct from a primarily personal or individualistic view of Christian salvation, has crossed the seas from South America to other lands and has influenced many who have hesitations about a full-blown version of Liberation Theology, with an explicit endorsement of violence (when no other means are available) and a readiness to ally itself with Marxists. So the pietistic kind of Christianity, which many Evangelicals and Catholics have tended to endorse, has given ground in Britain, as elsewhere, before a kingdom theology. 'Getting to heaven' or 'saving my soul' has been seen as part of a larger purpose: building the kingdom of God. This is true even of many Evangelicals, especially the influential evangelical party in the Anglican Church. A new emphasis on the teaching of Jesus in the Gospels and of the Old Testament prophets has been found to have a distinct relevance to modern society. In any case, an authentic witness to the gospel has been seen to include a witness to divine standards of morality: not only individual, but social. It is widely accepted that it is not enough simply to preach for individual conversions, to 'pluck brands from the burning'. To proclaim the gospel is to set before people the holiness of God, the demands of his moral law and the individual and social consequences of ignoring or disobeying it, as well as offering the remedy for moral failure through Jesus Christ. In doing that, the Church will necessarily take a position on many social, moral, ethical and even political issues. Faithfulness to the gospel, rather than a perverse desire to meddle in politics, is claimed to be the chief motivating force.

RENEWAL IN WORSHIP

Over the same period that saw these changes in the Church's approach to social issues, there has been a remarkable renewal in worship in the British Churches. It has affected almost all of them: those that have liturgies, and those that follow a less formal pattern of worship. A random survey of a dozen churches would be enough to illustrate these changes. There is much greater congregational participation, more emphasis on fellowship, more variety and flexibility. There is a great deal of new music, most of it simple and intended for congregational singing. But probably the distinctive difference, compared with, say, twenty years ago, is the *warmth* of the whole thing. For centuries the hallmark of British church worship was its coolness. It was all right to get excited at a football match; but in church restraint, dignity and self-control were to be preferred. But now, in all traditions, there has come an astonishing injection of enthusiasm in worship. People actually seem to enjoy it, and instead of scurrying silently away at the end, they are more likely to stay for a cup of coffee (or even, in some churches, a pint of beer).

Let me try to put some detail to these generalisations by taking four typical churches I know well, in different parts of the country, and in very different church traditions, and looking at the way their patterns of worship have changed over the past twenty-five years. None of them is by any means exceptional or unusual: in fact, I have chosen them most of all because they are broadly typical of what has happened.

Church A is a Roman Catholic parish church in the Home Counties, served by a monastic order with the help of a local community of nuns. Twenty-five years ago the Mass was in Latin; most of the music was plainsong or hymns rather unenthusiastically sung. The accompaniment was by organ. The congregational participation was minimal: a few set responses (in Latin), the Hail Mary, the Creed, the Our Father. At many Masses there was no sermon (or homily, as Catholics call it) and the general atmosphere was of a colourful but fairly arcane ceremonial, dignified and impressively reverent, but one to which the worshippers, many of whom did not receive Communion, seemed almost superfluous.

Today the Mass is in English, apart from an occasional celebration in Latin. The music is from a parish-grown collection of hymns and songs, most of which, at the main Sunday Masses, are accompanied by guitars, wind instruments and a little gentle percussion. The congregation is involved from first to last—in the songs and hymns, in the responsorial psalms in the Gelinau version, in reading the lessons and leading the intercessions, and in the 'peace', when worshippers greet each other, some with a handshake, some with a kiss or hug. The homily is brief, by protestant standards, based on the lectionary readings, and delivered in a quiet, informal style by one of the priests. Communion is distributed by the priests and by several lay helpers, men and women—they are called 'extraordinary ministers of Holy Communion'. The whole event is marked by warmth, enthusiasm, involvement and a sense of commitment.

All of this is consistent with the changes introduced by the Second Vatican Council. The section on the Eucharist quite clearly shifts the emphasis away from a solitary priest offering the holy sacrifice, towards a communal action of the people of God, 'the royal priesthood', involving everyone present, the priest representing the priesthood of all the faithful as he, in their name, offers *their* sacrifice to God. In theory the Roman Catholic doctrine of the Mass has not changed in a single detail since the Council of Trent. In practice the emphasis has altered so radically that the service as experienced by the worshipper has been transformed. The Eucharist has, in effect, been given back to the people.

Not all of the people have wanted it, of course. Some have even ceased to practise, regretting bitterly the absence in the modern service of what they describe as mystery, awe and reverence. Some (a few thousand, at most) have sought out the handful of places where the old Tridentine Mass is still celebrated. But most Catholics have come to appreciate and enjoy the 'new' service, and in the many congregations where there is a charismatic element the freedom to use extempore prayer and modern songs and hymns is fully exploited. The parish in question is one such, though the distinctive manifestations of the charismatic movement—tongues and prophecy—are usually confined to a mid-week meeting.

Numbers at Mass now are actually higher than twenty-five

years ago, which is against the national trend but consistent with the situation in other denominations in the churchgoing Home Counties. During the week there is a central prayer gathering, with a charismatic flavour, and many people also join in house groups or prayer-cells—probably a third of the 600 or so weekly communicants.

Church B is an Anglican parish in an urban priority area in the north-west of England. Twenty-five years ago it had a viable, if predominantly elderly congregation, most of them white working-class people who had lived all their lives in the area and appreciated the church's protestant and evangelical tradition. The services were strictly Prayer Book. The choir led the congregation through the set psalms and canticles of Morning and Evening Prayer. The sermons were substantial, the hymns traditional, the decor plain, if not stark (only the collection plate shone out from the varnished wooden holy table—there was no cross). The congregation were faithful, well instructed and generous: the church contributed substantially to overseas and home missions.

But it was the end of an era. As the elderly members grew too frail to attend church and one by one made their last visit there to the ringing words of the Prayer Book burial service, no one replaced them. The area's run-down Victorian housing was being abandoned by the old working-class people and taken over by the new Commonwealth immigrants. The new high-rise council flats were filled with families with problems: as the vicar put it, 'If they didn't have problems before they came, six months in that setting ensured they soon acquired them.' The congregation dwindled almost to nothing, and of those remaining, most were people who travelled several miles by car from the suburbs where they now lived.

But the church has not died. The seventies saw a determined effort to make the church's activities and worship more accessible to the people who actually live in the parish. A toddlers' club brought in the young mothers. A youth club, partly financed by the council, has created a link—sometimes tenuous, sometimes traumatic—between the church and some of the local youngsters. A policy of encouraging indigenous leadership has brought a number of black families into the congregation, and their presence is reflected in the style of worship. A family service, with only a loose framework betraying its roots in Anglican liturgy, is the main Sunday service.

Numbers are about the same as twenty-five years ago, but the average age of the congregation has fallen by about thirty years. So far attempts at persuading people to come to Bible study or prayer groups mid-week have not been very successful. Only the handful of professional people in the congregation—a couple of teachers, a young accountant— are really keen on the idea. The vicar works hard, probably too hard, and progress is slow. It is the archetypal *Faith in the City* parish, yet its members seem less concerned with questions of social justice than their counterparts twenty miles down the road in the affluent suburban churches. The charismatic movement is not really evident, but the worship has a freedom of its own.

Church C is a Baptist Church in a small midlands town. It is situated right in the town centre, a stone's throw from the shopping precinct—a prime site for the developers, though so far the church officers have resisted the temptation. Twenty-five years ago it was a prosperous little church of about 150 members, just celebrating its sixtieth anniversary.

In those days, like many Free Churches, it drew an eclectic congregation. Many of the church families had worshipped there for several generations and continued to attend even though they had moved away from the immediate area. As the only Baptist Church in the town, it drew loyal Baptists from a dozen neighbouring villages. The deacons—all men— were pillars of the local community. They always wore dark suits on Sundays and made an impressive sight when they sat together at the front, flanking the minister, at the monthly Communion service. The women all wore hats. The children were well scrubbed and fresh-faced. The choir—quite a good one—was predominantly female. The organist was competent if a bit heavy-handed.

There was no doubt about the central point of the service: the sermon. The layout of the church (all lines meeting at the pulpit) and the pattern of the service (everything preceding the sermon was likely to be called 'the preliminaries' by the deacons) emphasised the priority. The congregation had come to hear the word of God, and everything else was secondary. Indeed, the congregation was virtually silent apart from singing, with commendable gusto, four or five standard hymns. The minister's prayers were rounded off with his own solo 'Amen', while the worshippers sat in mute rows, some crouching and shading their eyes in an 'attitude of prayer', and others sitting immovably bolt upright. Signs of emotion, enthusiasm or ecstasy were rarely visible, and probably unwelcome. The word that naturally springs to mind to describe the church would be 'solid'—solid doctrine, solid teaching, solid people. It is not meant to be a criticism to say that a line from one of their favourite hymns more or less sums up this staunch body of believers: 'But nothing changes here'.

Yet it has. Somewhere in the intervening twenty-five years something quite revolutionary must have happened. The solid deacons of the 1960s have been replaced by be-sweatered young enthusiasts—men and women. The choir is now a large music group, with guitars, keyboards and drums. The old pipe organ has gone. So have the varnished pews. So have the old hymn books. So has the massive old pulpit, which dominated the interior of the building and set its occupant on a towering pinnacle of omniscience.

But the main change is not in these incidentals. It is in the congregation. 'Mute' is definitely *not* the word to describe them. The whole service is punctuated by a positive torrent of 'Hallelujahs' and 'Praise the Lords'. The air is full of waving arms, hands extended to the heavens. Ecstasy is everywhere. There is much embracing and hugging, many outward protestations of love and fellowship, a lot of laughter, too, and sometimes tears. The whole church seems to wear its collective heart on its sleeve.

The service is not without form, but at first it is hard to detect it. The opening consists of a long sequence of songs, many of them simple repetitions of phrases from the Bible ('Thou art my God and I will praise Thee') or bland devotional doggerel: 'We really want to thank you, Lord. We really want to bless your name. Hallelujah! Jesus is our King. . . ' This singing may go on for half an hour or more, with a marked rise in intensity and fervour, the songs becoming more serious, with a growing air of expectancy. Then, under the minister's direction, there is a time of testimony and praise—at first, simple accounts of blessings and answers to prayer during the past week, many of them to the outsider slightly banal and even trivial; then someone will speak in tongues, followed by an interpretation, and the atmosphere changes. A man gets to his feet with a prophecy; God has a word for his people about their failure to open their hearts to his gifts. The message is unremarkable: it is the medium that makes it special. The prayers that follow it pick up the images and ideas of the prophecy and a kind of theme for the service begins to emerge.

Eventually the Bible is read—it has been much quoted, sometimes out of context, but not read in a consecutive way until that point. After that the minister preaches: a powerful, personal 'message' (the old word seems exactly the right one to describe it), the exegesis a bit chancy but the passion carrying it along. The word of God is certainly applied to the life of the congregation and even, in a tangential way, to the life of society as a whole. But the talk, and indeed the whole service, is essentially about personal salvation, personal spiritual well-being, personal blessing. The word 'I' is ubiquitous, and God is generally invoked as a problem-solver or a giver of experiences. This rather contrasts with the earlier worship, which, whatever its aesthetic short-comings, was centred in worship of a holy God, 'high and lifted up'. So it is interesting that when the prayer and prophecy ends, and people with particular needs are invited to come forward so that members of the church can pray over them, the music swells up again in *worship*: 'Holy, holy, holy is the Lord; Holy is the Lord God almighty! Who was, and is, and is to come! Holy, holy, holy is the Lord!'

The actual number of people present is not much greater than twenty-five years ago, though the social and age composition is very different. This congregation is markedly younger, more metropolitan and less rural; probably better educated and certainly more affluent. In terms of impact on the town, the present-day church is undoubtedly better placed to reach people, and outsiders who came to the services would not find them as culturally alien as the old services must have seemed to non-churchgoers twenty-five years ago. However, not many of the members have been converted from complete unbelief through this church's ministry. Most were at least nominal churchgoers before they joined, and the ingredient they mostly suggest attracted them is the warmth or the reality of the services or the fellowship.

Church D is the civic, town-centre Anglican parish church of a well-to-do London suburb. Most of the houses in the parish now cost over £100,000, which means that most of the parishioners are either very well paid younger men and women, or older people who came to the district before house prices escalated. Twenty-five years ago the church was mainly noted for its choir, of almost cathedral standard. Matins was sung every Sunday morning, beautifully. And the church was full. The great and good of the district came. Lovers of church music (and architecture—it is a fourteenth-century-building) came and brought their friends. People who valued tradition, dignity and quality came. And people came because their parents had come, and because it was the 'decent' thing to do.

It is easy to ridicule the formal worship of an earlier era. In fact, it had many excellent, unitive elements. It did create a worshipping centre to a community. It did offer God worship and praise in some of the best words and music mankind has yet found for the purpose. And it did teach many generations a Christian ethic, based on the Bible, the Ten Commandments and the Sermon on the Mount. But it was not, generally speaking, a gospel-centred Christianity.

Today that church, too, has changed. In this case, the changes have been painfully, sometimes traumatically, carried through. When a new incumbent tried to introduce fresh ideas—largely to make the worship more congregational and less like a sacred concert—the organist and choir resigned *en bloc*. Others left because of changes in the pattern of services, the introduction of modern-language liturgy, and, finally, the reordering of the church interior.

That reordering was typical of much that has happened in Anglican and Roman Catholic churches over the last twenty-five years. The traditional parish church, either dating from the Middle Ages or a good imitation, expresses very vividly the theology of medieval Christianity. The body of the people are in the nave, spectators of the holy mysteries to be enacted in the chancel and the sanctuary. To emphasise the distinction, there was often a screen of wood or metal across the front of the chancel, to separate clergy and choir from lay people.

A further barrier, the altar rail, then effectively separated the choir from the priests and servers who carried out the ritual of the Mass before the altar.

The altar itself was either against the east wall of the church, or, in some churches, was a 'high altar' towering over chancel and nave, to be approached from all directions up a flight of steps. In any case it was remote from the congregation, and intentionally so. While not generally going as far as the Orthodox churches, where the central acts of the liturgy are carried out behind screens, with only the rising smoke of the incense and the singing of the priests to let the congregation know that anyone is still there, the pre-Reformation Church clearly did not feel that the vulgar eyes of the laity should feast upon the sacrament.

At the Reformation in England Cranmer tried to bring about a change. His Prayer Book seems to suggest (it is a subject of some dispute) that the Communion table, as he carefully called it, should be set 'lengthways' in the chancel, rather than altar-wise against the east wall, with the celebrant not standing with his back to the people—in what is called the eastward position—but at the north side of the table, presumably sideways on to them. Whatever Cranmer intended plainly did not happen, or did not survive for long. The inate conservatism of incumbents and their congregations probably saw to that, and the revival of traditional ritual and order under Archbishop Laud in the 1630s ensured that England's parish churches returned to their pre-Reformation layout.

So it remained until this century. Indeed, the Oxford movement positively gloried in chancel screens and high altars and all the paraphernalia of the sanctuary. Largely due to its influence, the rather quaint north side position, in which the celebrant stood sideways on to the congregation at the end of the Communion Table all but disappeared. By World War II the vast majority of English clergy adopted some variation of the eastward position at Communion, and almost every church had an altar-style Communion table standing against the east wall of the church, fenced in by altar rails, with the length of the chancel keeping the congregation at a decent distance.

The movement for liturgical renewal—which began between the wars and was known in Britain as 'Parish and People'—began the process of change in Anglican parishes. The new insights into eucharistic worship from Dom Gregory Dix took a long while to filter down to the local church, but eventually they arrived. The Second Vatican Council, which, as we have seen, transformed Roman Catholic worship, eventually persuaded all but the most entrenched Anglo-Catholics that liturgical renewal was not a protestant plot. Slowly at first, but then with gathering momentum, altars were moved away from the wall and set somewhere adjacent to the congregation, often in the nave or at the front of the chancel. The celebrant—now to be known as the 'president'—faced the congregation. Screens were either removed, if the archdeacon could be persuaded to grant a faculty, or simply rendered irrelevant by moving the whole ceremony in front of them.

The lay people were suddenly confronted with a dilemma. Did they actually *like* all this involvement? It was one thing to come to a sung Eucharist, watch from afar in reverent silence, make their Communion as inconspicuously as possible, and then slip away. But now they were actually expected to join in: to say and sing things, to be part of the action, even—horror of horrors—to shake hands with each other at the exchange of the peace.

Amazingly, most people decided over a period of time that they approved of the changes. Indeed, the constant decline in the number of weekly communicants in the Church of England was arrested: the figure actually rose in the eight years following 1976 (the period when the new *Alternative Service Book* came into use) from 635,000 to 703,000. But of course there were those who hated the changes, and *Church D* is exactly the sort of place you would expect to find them. When the chancel was opened up, and a free-standing nave altar installed, there were those for whom that was the last straw.

However, despite that opposition, there is now an enthusiastic congregation—not as large as in the balmy days of sung Matins, back in the 1950s, it is true: but much more committed. The spirituality of the parish is that of Taizé.[1] There is much prayer, and that prayer is related to the concerns of the community and of the world. The ministry is liberal in the best sense of that word: broad in its sympathies, undogmatic and open, and the worship is alive. In contrast to the times of its past glories, the congregation is younger, less formal and more willing to be involved between Sundays. *Church D* is probably typical of thousands of Anglican parishes all over England.

My four representative churches are not truly representative, of course. To make the picture anything near complete one must include the changes in the Churches of the Reformed tradition—the Presbyterians and Congregationalists—as well as the Methodists and the Anglo-Catholics. The Reformed Churches have also accepted some of the insights of liturgical renewal, though probably to a lesser extent than the other denominations. Apart from the relatively few congregations of a charismatic kind, most churches have experienced change, mainly in a greater emphasis on sacramental worship. There was a time when Communion in the great Presbyterian Churches was celebrated only once a quarter, with enormous emphasis on preparation for right reception. Today, many Churches have moved towards a monthly, or even weekly, celebration. But metrical psalms are still sung, and there is still a tradition of substantial sermons; the traditional layout of the church, with the dominant pulpit and the elders' chairs behind the communion table, is mostly undisturbed.

The sacramental trend is also noticeable in Methodist worship, along with a more adventurous approach to music, drama and liturgical dance than one finds in the Reformed Churches.

The Anglo-Catholics, as I have suggested already, have mostly absorbed the ideas of the liturgical movement. Some have also been profoundly affected by charismatic renewal. In fact, probably the best book on worship in a charismatic setting has come from a leading Anglo-Catholic bishop, Michael Marshall.[2] It is now quite rare to find a church where

---

[1] The ecumenical community in France that has sought to marry catholic and protestant spirituality.
[2] Michael Marshall, *Renewal in Worship* (Marshalls, 1982).

the altar is separated from the people or where the priest celebrates from the eastward position.

Renewal in worship, as I have said, has been remarkable and widespread. Like the changing attitude to social concern, it has its roots in theology, but that cannot alone account for its astonishingly wide acceptance. It arrived at the right moment. The 'cool' worship so typical of British religion was looking increasingly irrelevant to contemporary churchgoers. The 1960s—'swinging sixties' as they were dubbed—had liberated many people from emotional inhibitions. It was now acceptable for people to get excited about soccer, sex and showbiz. The restrained handshake of greeting had given way to the continental kiss. Even footballers could be seen week after week on the television in tears of ecstacy or frustration, or hugging and kissing each other when a goal was scored.

The churches of Britain could not hold back the tide for ever. The new insights of the liturgical renewal met a new desire for less formality and restraint, for more warmth, emotion and even passion. They made common cause. People began to clap in church, on suitable occasions—welcoming a new bishop or vicar, or responding to a visiting guest. The giving of the peace more or less obliged them to shake hands, at least, and some went further, hugging and kissing in a most un-English way. Then, as the more relaxed music came in, congregations sometimes responded by clapping in time with the rhythm, or lifting their hands up in worship. In fifteen years, no more, the face of worship in England changed irreversibly.

Mind you, it is still quite a shock to sit in a Eucharist in Westminster Abbey, the service sung by that splendid choir with all appropriate dignity, among a distinguished-looking congregation in their Sunday best and surrounded by the relics of our national glory, and suddenly find the place buzzing with animated conversation, with all these apparently private people thrusting their hands towards you and offering you 'the peace of the Lord'. But it is, for most of us, a pleasant shock, emphasising that Christian worship is an expression of unity and fellowship as well as beauty and dignity, and that this is as true when it takes place in a national shrine as when it is celebrated in a charismatic house group.

I have described this development as irreversible, and I

believe that it is. After all, a whole generation of younger worshippers has no experience at all of the old ways of doing things. When they do encounter them, they find them remote, obscure and unrewarding. Those of us who grew up with the quiet beauty of the *Book of Common Prayer* may wish it were not so, but as a vehicle of public worship it is no longer relevant—indeed, by the criteria of its own creator, Cranmer, it was long overdue for renewal. Alterations to the Church's liturgy, he argued in the preface to the *Book of Common Prayer*, are justified 'for the more proper expressing of some words or phrases of ancient usage in terms more suitable to the language of the present times . . . in such a language and order as is most easy and plain for the understanding both of the readers and hearers.'

The process is also irreversible because British Christianity is not now what it once was, and probably can never be again. The presence of perhaps half a million black Christians, with their own style of uninhibited worship, and of perhaps another half a million charismatic Christians in both mainstream and House Churches more or less guarantees that the temperature of worship will not fall. The pendulum may—probably will—swing back slightly towards order, certainly in the older Churches, but it is hard to believe that it will ever return to where it was twenty-five years ago.

MISSION

Just after World War II the Church of England published a report entitled *Towards the Conversion of England*. Largely the brain-child of the Bishop of Rochester, C M Chavasse, it was an eloquent and forceful call to the Church to recognise England as a mission field and accept the responsibility of evangelising it. Its definition of evangelism was to become widely accepted: 'Evangelism is so to present Christ Jesus in the power of the Holy Spirit that men may come to put their trust in him and serve him in the fellowship of his Church.' Its causal element is fascinating. Evangelism is defined by its results: it is '*so to present . . . that . . .*'. Presumably, therefore, evangelism has not taken place if no one has responded. In classical theology, on the other hand, to evangelise is simply

to proclaim the gospel. A community is said to be 'evangelised' when it has heard the good news of Jesus Christ. The
results of that proclamation are the concern of the Holy Spirit.

Whatever its intentions, the results of that Anglican report
were minimal. For all its sense of commitment and urgency,
it proposed few practical steps, and the Church provided in
response very few resources. It was strong on oratory but
weak on action. The Church had been wary of direct evangelism for a long while—more or less since the Wesleyan
split—and it was to be a few more years yet before any
significant part of the Church's leadership would put real
heart into mission.

But the report did represent one important change, in its
recognition of the need for mission. This was undoubtedly in
large part a response to serious lessons learned during the
war, particularly by service chaplains. There the extent of the
gulf between ordinary people (especially men) and organised
religion became starkly clear. But so did the fact that they
were not irreligious. Faced with danger and death, forced to
see how fragile a thing life itself is, they often turned to
religion for reassurance. It was then that the gulf yawned.
The language of the services (Anglican and Free Church) and
of the Bible (invariably in those days in the Authorised
Version) was unfamiliar and obscure. So was the whole style
of church worship.

In fact, a similar discovery had been made by a group of
chaplains thirty years earlier, in World War I, among them
Milner White, later Dean of York and a pioneer between the
wars in the field of liturgical revision. But such lessons are
absorbed only slowly, if at all, and it took a second 'wave'
to release a desire for change that could not be resisted.

So the immediate post-war years saw a great deal said and
written about communicating the gospel, about opening the
Churches to new influences, about bringing the people of
Britain back to God. There were notable evangelistic missions
in the late forties, in London and Scotland particularly, but
the predominantly liberal theology of the thirties, which still
prevailed among the clergy, inhibited them from whole-
hearted proclamation, and the Evangelicals were largely to
be found in those days in mission halls and para-church
organisations like the National Young Life Campaign. Conse-

quently there was a great deal of fragmented and often individualistic effort, but little of a co-ordinated kind and nothing
that made a national impact. However, something *was*
happening, especially through teams of Christian ex-
servicemen who brought back to civilian life the enthusiastic
fellowship they had enjoyed (often overseas) during the war.
Some of those men went on to train for the ministry, while
others created a network of potential support for evangelism
which was to prove invaluable in the following years.

The spate of new translations of the Bible in the post-war
period was evidence of concern to communicate the faith to
a wider range of people. J B Phillips' brilliant paraphrases of
the New Testament came like a light in a dark room to young
Christians like myself struggling to make sense of St Paul's
Epistles. The Revised Standard Version crossed the Atlantic
successfully, and subsequent decades have seen the New
English Bible—perhaps, in retrospect, a bit of a damp
squib—the Jerusalem Bible, the Good News Bible and the
New International Version. Sales of all of them were spectacular, evidence at least of a public interest in, if not hunger
for, religious truth.

The Billy Graham Crusades of the 1950s pointed in the
same direction. It is easy, over thirty years later, to romanticise
their effect. But they were high-profile, in a way Christianity
had not been for decades, and they made evangelism respectable, without making it boring—quite an achievement.

I was at the opening night of Graham's first Crusade in
Britain, at Harringay Stadium in North London—three miles
from my home—in March 1954. The young American evangelist had already attracted the attention of the media. London
was positively garish with strident blue and yellow posters,
and he had been denounced by prominent Labour politicians
for an alleged remark about the damaging effects of 'years of
socialism' in Britain. Graham had quickly explained that what
he had said (or written, or meant—the memory is confused)
was 'years of *secularism*'; not quite the same thing. At any
rate, the press turned up on the opening night to give this
young transatlantic upstart a roasting. But if they had come
to demolish, they stayed to praise.

The conversion of the media was of Damascus-road
proportions. All the popular papers the next morning made

Graham front-page news, many of them with banner head-
lines and large pictures. They had not sent their Religious
Affairs reporters. In any case, most of them had not got one.
Some sent their show-biz critic, some a sports writer, several
their gossip-columnists. One distinguished weekly sent the
Poet Laureate, John Betjeman. But whoever went, the result
was the same: virtually unanimous approval. I think they had
expected blood on the sawdust, hell-fire preaching and ranting
eloquence. What they got was good, standard evangelical
preaching of a conservative kind, but sensitively packaged:
quite a lot of humour and self-deprecation, illustrations drawn
from the current world scene, and the recurring refrain, 'the
Bible says . . . '. What actually impressed them most was none
of these, but the appeal—restrained, by American standards,
but clear and insistent—and the immediate, quick, dignified
response to it, as though hundreds of people had been waiting
in the shadows, instantly ready to walk out to the front and
receive Christ.

Most of the journalists had seen nothing remotely like it
before. They would admittedly have had to search hard for
it in London, but it certainly existed. Evangelists like Tom
Rees, preachers like Colin Kerr and Alan Redpath were saying
and doing much the same thing with much the same emphasis
week after week. But the world and his wife were not rushing
to hear them (though Rees managed to fill the Royal Albert
Hall pretty regularly), and certainly the media were not
beating a path to their door.

Graham's Greater London Crusade lasted right through
March and April. Only on the second night was there a single
empty seat in Harringay Stadium, which held about 14,000.
The closing rally was at Wembley Stadium, where a crowd
of something like 100,000 included the Archbishop of Canterbury, Dr Fisher, giving a belated establishment seal of
approval to the American evangelist. Tea at Buckingham
Palace with the Queen, and a visit to the Prime Minister, Sir
Winston Churchill, confirmed that approval. Those leading
churchmen—and they were a small band—who had risked
their reputations in backing Graham's Crusade in advance of
the event were entirely vindicated.

Billy Graham was manifestly very excited at the way things
had gone. With characteristic optimism he said that he

believed 'revival' was 'just around the corner' for Britain. It
has, one is forced to say, remained obstinately around that
same corner ever since, though each Graham campaign (and
there have been half a dozen since) has heard the same claim.
Whatever revival is—and I am not sure it is easy to define—
it does not seem to be the same thing as effective evangelism.
Graham raised the visibility of Christianity in Britain in 1954,
and he has repeated that achievement on every subsequent
visit. Undoubtedly many fringe Christians came to a living
faith through his meetings, and some people from completely
outside the Church community were brought to Christ. But
the church membership statistics tell their own story. For all
the vast numbers who attended Crusade meetings in the mid-
fifties, the overall membership of the Churches—*all* the
Churches—continued to decline. For each one who was
added, someone, through death or withdrawal, was taken
away. By the end of the fifties many Christians realised that
big missions, while excellent means of focussing attention on
the gospel, were not the best answer to the evangelisation of
Britain.

Oddly, the most significant effect of those Crusades was
almost certainly their impact on the Church of England. The
evangelical party had been a small and rather defensive
element in the Church since the 1930s, lacking in dynamic
leadership and often appearing more concerned to win arguments about ritual or liturgy than to evangelise the nation. It
may be coincidence, but the period immediately following the
Graham Crusades saw a sudden spurt in the number of young
men of an evangelical persuasion offering for the ministry.
All at once, evangelical theological colleges were bursting at
the seams. At the same time, clergymen who had bravely
taken the lead in inviting Billy Graham, and had been vindicated, felt able to assume a role of leadership among Anglican
Evangelicals. The Bishop of Barking, Hugh Gough, was the
only bishop to back Graham before his arrival. Among his
supporters were Maurice Wood, then Vicar of Islington, and
John Stott. Both were destined, in their different ways, to
exercise a profound influence on evangelicalism in the Church
of England over the next thirty years.

The revival—and that is surely not too strong a word—
of the evangelical cause in the established Church over that

period began in the mid-fifties, and I have little doubt that Billy Graham was a major human element in it. He gave confidence to the diffident, redirected the priorities of those who were preoccupied with ecclesiastical skirmishing, and demonstrated the possibilities of a gospel-centred ministry. So, if he himself did not bring the nation back to God, he at least brought a large part of the Church of England back to the gospel.

In the Free Churches, too, the Graham Crusades had a major impact—especially on his fellow Baptists. Again he was an influence for a more conservative message, but in a contemporary dress. He certainly made the gospel caravans and awkward street-corner open-air meetings look amateur and even gauche. A number of outstanding Baptist preachers such as Alan Redpath, Stephen Olford and Godfrey Robinson were to flourish in Graham's wake. The Free Churches of a more liberal tradition (the Methodists, Congregationalists and Presbyterians) were also affected by the Crusades, especially by the formation of specific evangelical groups in the denominations, and by a rise in the number of ministerial candidates who took a generally evangelical position.

However, as we have seen, the Graham Crusades did not solve the problem of mission. They appeared to propose a glamorous, instant and relatively painless way of evangelising the nation, but the nation remained unevangelised. While many evangelical ministers emulated Billy Graham in the pulpit, and took to urging their slightly bemused hearers to 'get up out of their seats' and come forward to confess Christ, other less favourable reactions occurred. Among another set of Evangelicals a neo-Calvinism took over, possibly in reaction to what they saw as 'man-centred' evangelism. By the 1960s this was a major influence in many university Christian Unions, and the chief spokesman of the movement, Dr Martyn Lloyd-Jones, of Westminster Chapel, was widely lionised. His Westminster Fellowship drew large numbers of mostly young, mostly Free Church ministers, and some of them adopted an openly hostile attitude towards mass evangelism. Their theology emphasised God's call rather than human response: Graham, they felt, reversed the emphasis.

The other negative reaction was from some non-Evangelicals. Many of them regarded mass evangelism as positively dangerous, encouraging Christians to see their mission as saving individuals (often at enormous financial cost) rather than transforming society. They also deplored what they saw as a revival of obscurantism in the way the evangelist and his followers used the Bible. Indeed, although Billy Graham specifically denied that he was a fundamentalist, some of his preaching in those days, especially on the creation stories and on the Second Coming, was indistinguishable from fundamentalism. Certainly it was enough to evoke a long and heated controversy in *The Times*. Its longer-term effect was to give a boost to those who held a conservative position on the Bible, and this was to be significant, as we shall see, in a gradual reshaping of the theological map of Britain over the following thirty years.

While argument has continued over the relative value of mass evangelism (which could perhaps be more accurately called 'big rally evangelism'), the emphasis, even among Evangelicals, has shifted towards a more church-based approach. There is now a much broader consensus on the importance of mission, and all the main denominations have training schemes and programmes aimed at church growth. But there is still no genuine consensus about the theology involved, though the need to invite a personal commitment (as opposed to regarding a person as a Christian solely on the basis of infant baptism) is now widely accepted among all groups, including Roman Catholics.

This paradox of an agreement about the need for mission but a disagreement about the content of the message is well illustrated in the story of the National Initiative in Evangelism (NIE) set up during Donald Coggan's time as Archbishop of Canterbury in the 1970s. A group of Evangelicals had been badgering the major church bodies to do something about evangelism. No one cared to say that it was not a priority, but equally no one seemed able to come up with an effective programme that would be widely supported. Some of the Evangelicals (though not all) wanted the denominations and the British Council of Churches to back a major nationwide mission headed by Billy Graham. Some of the more radical groups said quite openly that the gospel priority in the 1970s was to work for social justice in such festering problems as racism, poverty and bad housing.

When Dr Coggan became archbishop he put evangelism high on his own agenda, while also (in his 'Call to the Nation') asking questions about the kind of society that would reflect Christian values. The Nationwide Initiative was able to bring together Christian leaders of widely different views; it produced some excellent research into patterns of churchgoing; it supported several effective local projects and, for a while, kept evangelism on the general church agenda. Possibly related to this—who can tell?—there was in the seventies a much more determined attempt by many Churches at least to think about the needs of those on the fringe of, or completely outside, the organised religious life of Britain. Family services, guest services, 'welcome groups', house meetings and home study groups—all of these were signs of churches looking *out* rather than endlessly *in*. One statistical result has been a quite remarkable rise in adult baptisms in the Church of England, from 8,000 in 1970 to 40,000 in 1980. Clearly the Church was having some success in drawing into membership people whose background was not even nominally Christian— something that is probably unique since Britain was first evangelised.

However, the NIE was not, in itself, a success. Its most enthusiastic supporters eventually left in impatience at its inability actually to do evangelism (which was not, to be fair, its original remit). Its detractors dismissed it as a talking shop, or a sop to Evangelicals. In course of time those who believed in direct evangelism backed 'Mission England', with Billy Graham as its public spearhead, with quite a range of support from non-Evangelicals. Those who favoured a 'kingdom' theology kept aloof from what they saw as 'simplistic' solutions, though recognising that Graham's message itself had broadened over the years to take in many of the social implications of the gospel. In fact, some of the more effective agencies of Christian social involvement in recent years have been evangelical ones, notably the Evangelical Coalition for Urban Mission, the Shaftesbury Project and the Frontier Youth Trust. None of these could possibly be dismissed as narrowly pietistic, nor unconcerned with the application of 'kingdom' ethics to issues of justice and liberation.

UNITY

I have said that unity has been on the Churches' agenda, though less urgently than other issues. Perhaps this is not entirely bad news. The 1960s and 1970s saw several abortive attempts at unity between denominations, notably between Anglicans and Methodists and among the non-Roman Catholic Churches of Wales. Apart from the formation of the United Reformed Church, which brought English Presbyterians and Congregationalists into one body, these efforts have been fruitless. Real differences of theology—mostly over priesthood—have combined with an obstinate sense of inertia to frustrate the ecumenical enthusiasts. There have been documents and reports in plenty, and some, like those of the Anglican–Roman Catholic International Commission, have been very distinguished pieces of work. But it is hard to see much hope of progress towards unity in the present situation. Even a fairly innocuous covenant scheme between the major denominations sank in the sea of general apathy. A few church leaders are deeply committed to the ecumenical vision. A few are deeply suspicious of it. Most, to be honest, simply do not put it very high on their agenda. The great majority of churchgoers probably agree with them.

However, the results of the Lent project sponsored by the British Council of Churches in 1986, 'What on Earth is the Church For?', revealed a remarkable groundswell among ordinary churchgoers. Over 60,000 groups, with well over half a million members, took part in the five-week course, which was backed up by local radio stations. Those participating filled in a questionnaire about their beliefs and views. A computer analysis of these forms, published subsequently under the somewhat predictable title *Views from the Pews*,[1] showed that the great majority of those responding were in favour of intercommunion and were impatient at the lack of progress towards mutual recognition of ministries and sacraments. This was true of participants from Roman Catholic and Anglican Churches, as well as the Free Churches, though of course it has to be said that the participants in such projects tend to be the more ecumenically inclined.

---

[1] British Council of Churches, 1986.

Nevertheless, it is not impossible to imagine that British churchgoers are a bit sceptical about church unions (in the sense of uniting denominations) but have learned over several decades of inter-church co-operation locally that Christians really do have a great deal in common and ought to find ways of expressing it. Joint lay training schemes, united initiatives over matters of social and moral concern (Sunday trading, for instance, or abortion law reform) and support for Christian Aid Week have brought people together across the denominations. Equally the charismatic movement has been notably successful in bringing Christians together from catholic and evangelical backgrounds—even for worship. And, as we have seen, some major evangelistic campaigns have drawn support from different church traditions.

The result has been that the different groups of Christians in Britain know each other much better now than at any time since the Reformation. At the lay level there is a good deal of mutual respect and affection, and ministers in almost every area except Northern Ireland meet regularly in local fraternals. There is actually a good deal of friendly contact between priests and Protestant ministers even in Northern Ireland—after all, one Presbyterian minister caused a furore by fraternising with the Roman Catholic congregation over the road, but it was widely ignored that most of his congregation actually supported his actions. Certainly charismatic groups all over the Province regularly bring together Roman Catholics and Protestants in prayer and Bible study. Little of the real sectarian bitterness is between the genuinely committed members of the Churches of the Province, as was seen in the response of Christians from both communities following the bomb at Enniskillen on Remembrance Day 1987. It is the slogan-chanting hangers-on who seem to cause most of the problem, though some politically motivated priests and ministers have much to answer for in fuelling prejudice.

In any case, in the rest of the United Kingdom, and especially in England, there is a generally friendly atmosphere between the Churches, reflected at every level. Bishops and area superintendents and moderators meet regularly in most places, but so do the local clergy and the lay people. The difference from thirty years ago, for those of us who can remember, is very striking. I like to feel that religious broadcasting, which introduces people to the worship and beliefs of other Christians in a completely non-threatening context, has contributed to this. One feels that in the end this new atmosphere must produce visible results, though organisational unity, certainly between those churches with 'catholic' order and priesthood and the others, may be a long way off. The Inter-Church Process, begun in 1987, may change this, as we shall see later.

So the Church in the 1980s is in a fascinating state of transition. As statistics show, its numerical decline continues, though perhaps more slowly, and not evenly across all the Churches. Yet there is also fascinating evidence of a more positive kind. For four consecutive years up to 1987 there was an increase in the number of people applying for the Anglican ministry and being accepted for training. In the same period the Baptist Union reported a substantial growth in its membership, for the first time for some sixty years. Numbers of regular Church of England communicants rose roughly 10 per cent between 1976 and 1984, again after many years of decline. And both the Black-led Churches and the House Church movement reported steady growth in membership.

We need to look closely at all these figures before we accept them at face value—or, indeed, the figures of apparent decline. The picture is neither uniform nor consistent, as our more detailed analysis of the Church of England in the following chapter will show. But I think it is indisputable that the period of steady and predictable shrinkage in church membership is over, and that itself is highly significant.

Equally significant is the evidence already cited of a widespread interest in religious faith. Britain is neither 'heathen' nor 'secular'. Indeed, a noted sociologist in a book published in 1987 argues that we are experiencing in the modern world 'an outburst of religiosity unique in human history'.[1] The battle for the next decade or so, where the Churches are concerned, will be to draw that interest into committed membership. It will not be easy, but at least the signs are propitious. The Church is, at last, looking outwards—whether in mission or in social involvement—rather than inwards. Its leadership, as I shall argue later, is of a high

---

[1] Geoffrey Nelson, *Cults, New Religions and Religious Creativity* (Routledge, 1987).

calibre and commands considerable public respect. It has a well trained and highly motivated professional ministry, who are nowadays more strategically distributed across the various sectors of society. It is beginning to recognise and mobilise the large number of able and gifted women in its ranks—a resource wasted in most of the Protestant Churches since the Reformation. And it has a major foothold in the organs of communication, especially broadcasting.

All of this collectively does not, I agree, add up to proof of a religious revival, nor of an inevitable upturn in the fortunes of the Christian Church. But it does mean that the wind is blowing in the right direction.

CHAPTER FIVE

THE CHURCH OF ENGLAND

THE CHURCH OF ENGLAND IS THE CHURCH which the great majority of English people stay away from. That is not quite as crazy as it sounds. According to every opinion poll, more English people—40 per cent in a 1987 poll by Harris for TVam—describe themselves as 'Church of England' than all other religious groups added together. Yet less than 4 per cent of the total population attend Anglican services regularly. Almost all the other major Churches in Britain are better supported by their membership, yet the influence of the Church of England on national life is still considerable, probably greater than that of any other religious body in England. Only the Church of Scotland—the United Kingdom's other established Church—equals or surpasses its influence on the life of its own nation.

Thus it is not unreasonable, in a book about the Churches of Britain, to give particularly detailed attention to the Church of England. In this chapter I want to look at it in some detail in its present-day manifestation. Despite many detractors, both within and outside its ranks, it has refused to wither away. It still commands enormous attention in the media—more so now, as I have argued, than for many years in the past. Its leaders still have access to the places of power. Its plant—churches, halls, schools, colleges—still dominates the landscape. And once or twice a year, most notably at Christmas, a very substantial part of its nominal membership actually puts in an attendance at a service.

So the statistics do not tell the whole story about the Church of England, by any means. As a national Church, with a large fringe, it is more vulnerable than most to shifts and changes in fashion. But its core of committed membership seems to be more reliable than in the past, and its place in public esteem seems to be higher than in the pre-war or immediate post-war period.

In an attempt to get behind those statistics, and, as it were, take the Church's temperature and assess its general health, I have made use of an extensive survey, conducted in 1987 with the help of 150 parochial clergy. They were carefully selected to represent as accurate a cross-section of the clergy as possible, in geographical location, type of parish and age. This sample was itself checked against the profile of the national situation as revealed in official statistics, and adjusted where necessary. So I would claim that this is a reasonably accurate picture of the situation in the parishes of England, and of the views and attitudes of Anglican clergy. The full statistical result is given here, and I shall be referring to the findings, and to comments elicited from respondents, as I draw my sketch of the Church of England in the 1980s.

1987 Survey of Beneficed Clergy

Type of parish:

Rural	30%
Town	24%
Suburban	30%
Inner City	16%

Best attended weekly service:

Holy Communion	70%
Morning Prayer	7%
Family Service	21%
Evening Prayer	2%

Best attended annual service:

Christmas Midnight Communion	38%
Christmas Carol Service	21%
Harvest Festival	10%
Easter Communion	10%
Other	14%

Regular church attendance over the last five years:

Greater	72%
Fewer	14%
Same, or don't know	14%

Which liturgies are in regular use in your parish?

Book of Common Prayer	52%
1928 Prayer Book	16%
Rite A	85%
Rite B	23%
Other	18%

Which liturgy is used at your principal communion service?

Book of Common Prayer	12%
Rite A	66%
Rite B	16%
Other	5%

Which liturgy would you use if it were your sole choice?

Book of Common Prayer	6%
Rite A	84%
Rite B	10%

Extent of involvement of women in leading worship:
Parishes where women

Read lessons	95%
Lead intercessions	92%
Administer the cup	47%
Are Lay Readers	19%

What vesture do you normally wear when celebrating Communion?

Surplice and scarf	10%
Surplice or alb and stole	34%
Eucharistic vestments	56%

Do you have organised house groups?

Yes	80%
No	20%

How would you describe your theological position?

Central	40%
Evangelical	26%
Anglo-Catholic	25%
Charismatic	17%
High Church	17%
Radical	16%
Other	16%

(Several gave more than one reply)

Extent of lay involvement in parochial ministry:
Churches where lay people

Teach in Sunday school	86%
Do visiting	77%
Lead house or prayer groups	73%
Lead youth clubs	73%
Do baptism preparation or follow-up	48%
Do marriage preparation or follow-up	16%

Churches with (lay) readers:

Yes	60%
No	40%

Do you feel Synodical government has benefitted the Church?

Yes	55%
No	36%

How would you describe your relationship with your bishop?

Supportive	28%
Encouraging	19%
Understanding	17%
Occasional	17%
Close	9%
Remote	7%
Unsympathetic	2%
Non-existent	1%

In general, which of these views do you adopt on political matters?

Social Democrat	34%
Conservative	25%
Liberal	16%
Labour/Socialist	16%
Multilateral Disarmament	44%
Unilateral Disarmament	14%
Nuclear Pacifist	14%
Pacifist	6%

Anglican Churches*

	Members	Ministers	Churches
Church of England	1,674,456†	12,722	16,632
Church in Wales	115,896	698	1,450
Church of Ireland	157,000	364	440
Scottish Episcopal Church	37,000	240	315
Totals	1,984,352	14,024	18,837

* Figures in this and later tables are from the UK Christian Handbook 1987/88 Edition, based on 1985 figures.
† Church of England figures include the Free Church of England and the Protestant Evangelical Church of England.

A HEALTHY HEART

The first thing to say is that the Church seems to be in relatively good heart. Whether one takes rural parishes (nearly 30 per cent of our sample), town (24 per cent) or inner-city (nearly 17 per cent), the majority claim that church attendance has increased over the last five years. This is most noticeable, surprisingly, in rural and inner-city parishes, and least evident in town churches. But the overall picture is of growth, even if of modest proportions. That, of course, mirrors the official statistics: regular Sunday communicants have risen by some 10 per cent since 1976, when such figures were first available. At the same time, usual Sunday attendances have remained more or less static, on the official figures—reflecting, I believe, a move towards less regular attendance by fringe members, perhaps at a monthly 'family service'.

Just as this picture of growth of committed members includes churches in all locations, so it includes churches of different theological traditions. But here, too, there is some variation. Growth is most common in churches whose ministry is described as 'evangelical' or 'charismatic' and least common in churches in the high church or Anglo-Catholic tradition. In fact, Anglo-Catholics record the largest percentage of churches with falling attendances (20 per cent), and charismatics the highest percentage of growing congregations (nearly 81 per cent). Obviously these figures depend on the incumbent's own perception of the situation, but where external checks could be applied the respondents were found to be commendably honest.

It is the pattern of churchgoing that has changed, but official statistics of membership, weekly communicants and weekly attendances largely miss it. Extrapolating the national figures on the basis of the parishes we surveyed, we discover an interesting picture. About 2.5 per cent of the population of England regularly attend Anglican services (and that means in practice every week). This more than doubles for the 'best attended service of the year'—Christmas midnight Communion or carol service, in most cases (over 60 per cent). It more than quadruples, no less, for those who come very occasionally, which in practice means once or twice a year. So, while only 25 people in a thousand are weekly Anglican churchgoers, 130 in a thousand go occasionally, and would, in the terms of our survey, regard the parish church as *their* church.

These figures relate solely to the Church of England. But there is no reason to suppose that the pattern is vastly different for the other mainstream non-Roman Catholic churches, and even the Catholic population is less inclined to regular and consistent Sunday Mass attendance than it used to be. Comparing our Anglican findings with general church statistics, we can reasonably assume that at Christmas something like 20 per cent of the population of England attend a church service and that perhaps twice that number are occasional churchgoers. The problem is the size of the fringe membership of other churches, which is mostly unrecorded. But my figures assume it is relatively smaller than the Anglican fringe, for reasons already given. It is hard to say whether a large fringe is a good thing for a church or not. What is certain is that more people are attached to churches, however loosely, and especially the Church of England, than normal membership statistics suggest.

One respondent added an interesting comment about church attendance. Answering the question, 'Is attendance greater or smaller?' he replied: 'No, it's much the same, but there is open acknowledgement that the *character* of the church has changed profoundly. There is a much more committed, active and united congregation. People now join us for positive religious reasons!' I believe his comment mirrors a widely recognised phenomenon, which shrinking statistics have tended to ignore. Sheer quantity is not everything—indeed, it may be next to nothing at all if attendance is for the wrong reasons. But the quality of church life, including the degree of enthusiasm which people bring to attendance at services, is highly significant. For one thing, it means that when the less committed person puts in his monthly or quarterly visit to church, he may well find the place alive and well, instead of moribund. There is a crèche, perhaps; a warm welcome at the door; well planned music and good, enthusiastic congregational participation in the service. And afterwards there is probably a cup of coffee. Twenty or thirty years ago, one has to say, it was not so.

FAMILY WORSHIP

Naturally, such things are not the only or the most fundamental innovations. The last two decades have produced
evidences of other marked changes in the life of the Church
of England. One of the most obvious is the continuing shift
towards a weekly Communion service as the central act of
parish worship. Some 70 per cent of our respondents gave
'Holy Communion' as the best attended weekly service. What
is slightly more surprising is that nearly 21 per cent have a
family service as the main weekly draw—especially when
many of the Communion services are in fact Family
Communion, also with children present and fully involved.
By comparison, Matins—once the archetypal Anglican
service—is the main service in only 7 per cent of parishes,
and Evensong ('The day thou gavest, Lord, is ended. . .') in
only 2 per cent.

Clearly this shift has been largely dictated by need. A
combination of the decline in Sunday schools and a desire to
draw into the life of the church not only children but their
parents, has persuaded clergy and church councils to cater
for families. So a very large number of churches run a crèche
for the babies and toddlers, and congregations in general have
learned (usually, but not always, with good grace) to accept
the presence of older children throughout the service. Modern
children are disinclined to be 'seen but not heard', so that the
reverent hush so beloved of former generations of Anglicans
is rapidly becoming a thing of the past.

But it is not just a matter of meeting a need. There is also
a theological principle involved. If the Church is the family
of God, then surely its principal service should involve all of
that family? So the Family Communion often sees a family
bringing the bread and wine to the altar and, later on, the
children coming up to the communion rail for a prayer of
blessing while the adults receive the elements. And the less
formal Family Service aims to involve children and adults in
a simple, cheerful and open form of worship.

There is always, however, a price to be paid. The Family
Communion more or less compels the preacher to be brief—
six or seven minutes seems to be the norm: too short, many
people feel, for the main teaching ministry of the week. It

also creates a rather restless, distracting environment for adult worship—though that is by no means the invariable result. Family Services are a proven success in drawing in fringers and attracting new churchgoers, especially young parents. But again the level of both teaching and worship is necessarily undemanding. It is possible for people to attend a monthly Family Service for years and never progress any further. There is also the obvious danger of confirming a widely held suspicion that Christianity is essentially for children rather than adults.

Neither objection is insuperable, but the advent of family-based worship *has* changed Anglican services. The traditional choral service—quiet, dignified, reverent—seldom succeeds in co-existing with the more popular, less formal family worship. Many clergy now face the problem of 'what next?' Where do you expect those brought up on choruses and simple talks with visual aids to go in search of more substantial spiritual fare? The battle now is to build bridges from the popular side to the more demanding fields of commitment and Christian maturity.

One answer emerges clearly from the survey. Some 80 per cent of the churches questioned have some kind of house groups—regular meetings for prayer, Bible study and fellowship. That is a remarkable figure, especially when one notes that almost 30 per cent of the sample consisted of rural parishes, where it might be thought very difficult to organise such groups.

The reason for them, I believe, is connected with an earlier observation about preaching. Given that the Sunday sermon is very brief, by traditional standards, there is obviously a need for the congregation to be taught the faith and guided in discipleship in some other way. House groups are a splendid way of doing this—informal, participatory, adaptable and relaxed; yet structured (often following a planned course of study) and really quite intense. Pastoral care is also simplified, since the group leaders are able to keep an eye on the six or eight members of the group in a way the vicar could never hope to do with the whole congregation. And often, in churches of all traditions, people also learn to talk about their faith and to experience prayer together in a way their parents and grandparents seldom did.

As Bishop Lesslie Newbigin of the Church of South India has written: 'The language of the New Testament simply cannot be applied to our huge gatherings. We absolutely require the development of a multitude of occasions when Christians can meet together in small groups, where they can know each other, listen to each other, pray for each other and bear each other's burdens. It is from such groups as these that real renewal can come to the Church.'[1]

There are dangers, too, of course. House groups depend on the availability of good leaders, and on a sound relationship between those leaders and the clergy. They can give rise to cliquishness, or even become little hotbeds of dissent or resentment in a parish. They can also become *too* intense, so that members feel spiritually blackmailed if they are not prepared to confess their sins publicly, or engage in this or that spiritual exercise.

But the advantages clearly outweigh the dangers, most of which can be avoided by careful pastoral oversight. Probably the selection and training of house group leaders is the single greatest priority in many parishes, and the presence of successful house groups the single most obviously identifiable factor in church growth: a quarter of the churches reporting nil growth or numerical decline had no house groups. In comparison, 88 per cent of growing churches had house groups.

CHURCHMANSHIP

Another major change is in the area of churchmanship. Few accurate surveys of this have been done, but there seems little doubt that forty years ago, most clergy would have described themselves as 'central'. The next largest grouping, by some distance, would have been the Anglo-Catholics. Evangelicals—and there is some statistical basis for this, at least—would have made up less than 10 per cent of the beneficed clergy.

According to our survey, the central group is still the largest—40 per cent. The numbers describing themselves as

---

[1] *Good Shepherds* (Mowbray, 1985), p. 80.

Anglo-Catholic or Evangelical are almost exactly equal in size, at 25 and 26 per cent. However, to the Anglo-Catholics one might not unreasonably add those who call themselves catholic (3 per cent) and high church (17 per cent), giving a total of 45 per cent. And to the Evangelicals one might equally reasonably add those describing themselves as charismatic (17 per cent), giving a total of 43 per cent. The totals come to more than 100 per cent because, not surprisingly, some clergy chose more than one label for their position.

What emerges is the picture of a Church with three substantial and very nearly equal theological groupings, central, catholic and evangelical/charismatic. Those describing themselves as liberal (4 per cent) or radical (16 per cent) were surprisingly few.

One comment has to be made on these figures. They relate to *incumbents*, men in charge of parishes, who are generally speaking older (predominantly forty-plus) and have been ordained at least six or seven years. One suspects that the trend towards an increasingly large evangelical/charismatic group in the Church would be more noticeable if younger clergy were included, as would the number of radicals, very probably.[1]

In any case, the figures show a real change. In the great sweep of Church history it is a fascinating one. It means that the two great movements to affect the Church of England after the Reformation settlement—the evangelical revival in the eighteenth century and the Oxford movement in the nineteenth century—have both had a profound and permanent effect on its life. There was a time in the 1930s and 1940s when one could easily have imagined the evangelical element in the Church either disappearing entirely or becoming a tiny congregationalist faction, with no influence at all on the development of Anglican doctrine or practice. There seems no likelihood today of such a situation.

But it is not simply a business of shading churches on the ecclesiastical map in terms of party groupings, for all the world like a political electoral graph. Obviously the edges of these labels have blurred. Many Anglo-Catholics describe

---

[1] This trend is even more clearly seen in lay church membership. The average electoral (membership) roll of evangelical parishes in the London diocese is 184. The comparable figure for the non-evangelical parishes is 92, exactly half.

themselves also as charismatic. Several clergy claimed to be 'evangelical Catholics' or 'catholic Evangelicals'. Perhaps more significantly, the old shibboleths have also blurred. In the 1950s an Evangelical was someone who wore cassock, surplice and scarf at Communion, stood at the north end of the Holy Table, and used nothing but the 1662 *Book of Common Prayer*. Today he is more likely than not to wear a stole when presiding at the Eucharist, almost certain to take the westward position and prefers the Rite A *Alternative Service Book* service to any others. The result is that it is not as easy as it once was to determine a church's theological stance from visual clues, nor even from the form of service used.

LITURGY

That is, in fact, a symptom of another profound change— the emergence of a new form of common prayer in a liturgy which has won the overwhelming support of almost all the clergy. Given the traditional idiosyncracy of the Anglican clergy, it is almost miraculous that 84 per cent of our respondents gave the ASB Rite A as the liturgy they would choose for Holy Communion if the decision were entirely their own. This preference was shared by those of every shade of churchmanship. I cannot imagine that any liturgy in the post-Reformation history of the Church of England has had quite such unanimous and enthusiastic support: certainly not since the late eighteenth century. It also says a great deal for the tolerance and sensitivity of the clergy that 52 per cent of them still regularly use the 1662 Prayer Book in their parishes and over 30 per cent do not yet have Rite A as their principal eucharistic liturgy.

In fact the liturgical revolution has occurred in the Church of England without evoking the storm of complaint some had feared. It is true that the Prayer Book Society has a vociferous membership, including a number of very distinguished people. But it is very small and seems to represent no coherent body of lay opinion. The new liturgies can be introduced only with the approval of the church council, an elected lay body. The fact that well over 80 per cent of the parishes questioned have one or other of the *Alternative Service Book* rites as their principal weekly Communion service suggests no great degree of lay resistance, at any rate from the committed membership. From time to time it is alleged that clergy have bullied councils into accepting change, or even ridden roughshod over their opinions, but several exhaustive attempts to find and examine such cases have failed to turn up a single convincing example.

That process of liturgical change was made possible only by the introduction of synodical government. The Liturgical Commission, it is true, was set up in 1954 and began work on the future revision of the Prayer Book. But previous attempts at revision, and notably that of 1928, had foundered on the spiky rocks of parliamentary approval. The introduction of synodical government in 1970 meant that future revision would only reach parliament for its approval after it had been shown to have the overwhelming support of the elected representatives of the laity, the clergy and the bishops in synod. And indeed it received that overwhelming support. As the long and (at times, it has to be said) tedious process of revision reached its final stages, so the votes became almost unanimous in its favour. I sat and watched several key debates and heard the pros and cons of various elements hotly debated. But, the debate over, and the odd point here and there having been graciously conceded, there was seldom the need for a formal division; the forest of hands in favour said it all. In 1980 the *Alternative Service Book* was published, and within a few months it was in widespread use, not only mopping up the congregations that had used the experimental Series 2 and Series 3 forms, but also advancing into those bastions of tradition, the cathedrals and choral foundations. It had taken the Church of England 318 years to revise its liturgy, but it took barely 318 days for most of the clergy and laity to show their enthusiasm for the new order.

Some, of course, were not enthusiastic about it. Probably many who were brought up on Cranmer have some nostalgia for the rolling cadences of the old book, for its dignity and theological consistency: even though they may find that theology rather narrow. But I do not know of any church which has introduced the new services and subsequently gone back to the old ones. Even those who are utterly opposed to the new services know in their hearts that opposition is a lost cause. I think one can safely say that the position is now irreversible, and that, for better or worse, the 1662 *Book of Common Prayer* will have disappeared from everyday parish use by the end of the century.

DOCTRINE

Liturgy has not been the only or main area of controversy in the Church, by any means. Equally significant has been the battle over doctrine. This has always been a source of contention in the Church of England—though it is hardly alone among the Churches of Christendom in that respect. In the sixteenth and seventeenth centuries the struggle was, broadly, between a protestant and a catholic view of the Church. But since the eighteenth century there has developed a strong liberal element in much Anglican theology, with a degree of scepticism about miracles and a generally rationalistic approach to questions about the existence and activity of God. After Darwin this element flourished, and the prevailing flavour of Anglican theology over the first half of this century was undoubtedly moderate liberalism. Without going as far as many of their counterparts on the continent, and especially in Germany, English theologians for the most part cultivated a degree of scepticism about traditional doctrine and poured elegant scorn on any notion of certainty or assurance about the content of the Christian faith.

The public stance of the Church of England, however, so far as its formal pronouncements were concerned, remained orthodox. Of course, given the nature of the Church, one would expect it to produce the occasional colourful bishop who would create a stir by challenging this or that traditional doctrine, or even, like the late Bishop Barnes of Birmingham, most of them at once. There have been several attempts at achieving in the field of doctrine the kind of revision so successfully achieved in liturgy, but the fate of the various reports on doctrine has been invariably the same: a spasm of generally negative criticism, and then oblivion. The latest report,[1] in 1981, was by general consent much the most

[1] Doctrine Commission of the Church of England, *Believing in the Church* (SPCK, 1981).

impressive, and response to it has been broadly favourable. But it would be a bold person who claimed that it had changed the actual beliefs of a single ordinary member of the Church of England.

Those beliefs remain stubbornly orthodox, to the extent that even clergy of definite liberal views tend to keep such ideas out of the pulpit. There is a general suspicion of fanaticism, but the core membership of the Church seems in no mood to tolerate any hanky-panky with the fundamentals of the faith.

That is the background to the extraordinary furore over some remarks of the newly appointed Bishop of Durham, Dr David Jenkins, in 1984. In a television interview, and then on the radio and in the press, he expressed doubts about the historicity of the Virgin Birth and of the empty tomb of Jesus and argued that in any case the latter did not matter as the heart of the Resurrection was a spiritual, not a physical, event. The media reacted as though something uniquely surprising, utterly unprecedented and appallingly shocking had occurred. There was, of course, no shortage of conservatively minded clergy on hand to denounce the bishop for heresy, and there were even calls for the Archbishop of York not to proceed with his consecration.

But Dr Jenkins *was* consecrated, giving the usual assent to Catholic doctrine as received by the Church of England. Shortly afterwards, however, the roof of York Minster, where the service had taken place, was struck by lightning and seriously damaged. Again, there was no shortage of people ready to see in that the hand of God, 'the Almighty getting His own back', as *The Times* put it.

The controversy rumbled on for almost two years until the bishops published a carefully worded and surprisingly unanimous report, *The Nature of Christian Belief*. This asserted categorically that belief in the virginal conception of Jesus, and that his tomb was empty on Easter morning, 'express the faith of the Church of England'. They left a lifeline for Bishop Jenkins, though. 'There must always be a place in the life of the Church', they said, 'for both tradition and enquiry.' If most of the bishops—all but two, according to one source—stood firmly on the side of tradition, there seemed little harm in allowing one or two others to venture on to the shifting sand of enquiry.

The bishops' report undoubtedly defused the situation. By and large it reassured the conservative majority (in the Church, and in synod) that the bishops were not about to compromise the historic faith. And it told those of more liberal views that they, too, could find a home in the Church. Whether they would in future find a home on the bench of bishops seems a more open question. The debate of the report in synod, despite a passionate speech by Bishop Jenkins, made it plain where majority sympathies lay. The clergy affirmed their belief in the Virgin Birth and the empty tomb with only one vote against. The vote in the House of Laity was 163 to 10. Modest theological speculation would be tolerated, but public denial of fundamental Christian beliefs, at any rate by bishops, was clearly not being encouraged.

The theological difference Bishop Jenkins highlighted in his synod speech, however, is not going to disappear overnight. He spoke scathingly of a 'laser-beam God' who could be called upon to intervene miraculously in various situations. Such a God, he claimed, was no more or less than an idol. His God, it seems, would not intervene in that specific way. If he would, why did millions die in Nazi gas chambers? A God who could intervene in such circumstances, but chose not to, would be 'the very devil'.

I doubt if synod, who received his speech warmly, in a generous mood of reconciliation, actually realised at the time how deeply offensive his argument is to orthodox Christians. It seems to imply that St Paul, St Augustine, Martin Luther, John Wesley, and millions of ordinary Christians down the ages, who believed in God's power to intervene miraculously in the human situation, in fact worshipped the devil. I doubt if he *did* mean that, but one of the problems about the Bishop of Durham is that he tends to get carried away with his own eloquence. He sees himself as a catalyst for change, who makes people think by setting out his ideas in bold and even shocking language. In fact, that approach—well suited to the university lecture hall, where he has spent almost all of his ministry—is as likely to create reaction as action in a church congregation. Certainly in this case it brought into being the most conservative document to emerge from the English episcopate since the Thirty-nine Articles were drawn up over 300 years ago.

In general, the Church of England's theology is demonstrably more conservative now than it was thirty or forty years ago. Half of the Church's theological colleges adopt a conservative and orthodox position. The bishops, as we have seen, are predominantly orthodox in their views. About half the ordinands each year are evangelical, and a further fifth are strongly catholic. The kind of optimistic liberalism that flourished between the wars has all but disappeared, except among some of the older clergy.

The radical challenge now comes from two different, and yet allied, quarters: the anti-dogmatic Christian anarchists, who write off the Church and most of its doctrine while professing great enthusiasm for a gospel-based theology; and the radical Evangelicals, who want to see orthodox, biblical Christianity used as a hammer to smash the mould of privilege and social injustice. Neither group is very large, though both tend to write a good deal to the Church press and attend conferences. But both also share an impatience with the ecclesiastical infrastructure and a burning desire to change the Church as a first step to changing society. Indeed, many would say that the Church as we know it must die, before a new Church and then a new community can emerge.

Most Anglicans have more modest aims: to keep the roof on, pay the 'quota' (the parochial contribution to central funds), offer decent worship to God and achieve a modest growth in numbers. They do not expect to bring in the kingdom of God or to overthrow the kingdom of Mammon. But (increasingly, I feel) they are aware of a sense of responsibility towards society as a whole. They do care about poverty, unemployment and bad housing, and many congregations have tried to do something about it. And they do want to share their faith with others, the Evangelicals more fervently than the rest.

ANGLO-CATHOLICS

The catholic party has been going through a fairly lengthy period of introspection. Articles, pamphlets and even a symposium have spoken of a 'crisis' in Anglican catholicism. This feeling of anxiety is associated, of course, with developments in the Anglican Communion that have seriously threatened several foundation principles of catholicity: liberal theology, women priests, pan-protestant ecumenism. The catholic party has become fairly isolated over several of these issues—notably the ordination of women to the priesthood. And this issue, more than any other, has made Anglo-Catholics question their continuing place in the Anglican Communion. Indeed, in the United States it has led to a minor (though very painful) schism, and there have been grave warnings that the same thing, but on a larger scale, might happen in England in similar circumstances. No less a figure than the Bishop of London, Graham Leonard, has compiled a dossier of priests and bishops who would rather separate themselves from their fellow Anglicans and form what amounts to a breakaway Church than continue to be part of a Church of England that ordained women to the priesthood. Such a body would not technically be in schism, because no one would be excommunicated and (so the plan goes) its clergy would still be in Anglican orders and under the jurisdiction of an Anglican bishop, even if he were no longer part of the 'college' formed by the House of Bishops.

The whole prospect seems dismal, self-defeating and confusing, and it has to be said that most clergy of the catholic wing of the Church of England recoil from it. Some may secede (and a few have already) to the Roman Catholic or Orthodox Churches. Most will undoubtedly remain in the Church of England, some with grave reservations, making use of various provisions to exclude women priests from their parishes. But many, probably a slowly growing number, are actually in principle in favour of the ordination of women to the priesthood and would have little difficulty in accommodating themselves to the new situation.

The ecumenical issue is now less threatening to Catholics. They headed the opposition to Anglican—Methodist reunion in the 1960s and 1970s, successfully denying two schemes the necessary two-thirds majority in each house of synod (the first vote was in the days of the Church Assembly). They were also less than ecstatic about the earlier formation of the united Church of South India, because some presbyters had not been episcopally ordained. 'Apostolic succession' is still a key issue for many Anglican Catholics.

But the ecumenical agenda of the 1980s and 1990s looks quite different. There is no serious proposal on the table, or even in the drafting room, for reunion between the Church of England and any protestant group. On the other hand, the quaintly named ARCIC (Anglican–Roman Catholic International Commission) has made considerable progress in establishing common theological ground between the two Communions and, were it not for the vexed issue of women priests, the prospects for some kind of eventual union between them would be good. Everything now seems to be in limbo, which is probably good news for the internal unity of the Church of England, if bad news for those of us who care for the visible unity of Christendom.

What is undeniable is that the catholic party has had an enormous influence on the worship of the Church of England. Well over half the clergy in our sample wear eucharistic vestments at their main Communion service; 160 years ago the figure would probably have been zero. That represents a remarkable transformation of the externals of Anglican worship, as does the introduction of such things as lighted candles, robed choirs, confessions, sanctuary lamps, reservation of the sacrament and the use of incense.

But the Church has stolen the Catholics' clothes without accepting Catholic doctrine. By no means every priest wearing vestments accepts the eucharistic doctrines traditionally associated with them. Indeed, many take refuge in the statement in the Church's revised Canons that it attaches 'no doctrinal significance' to the variety of vesture permitted by the measure. They are anxious to represent visibly the catholicity of their ministry, without endorsing Roman Catholic beliefs about transubstantiation or eucharistic sacrifice. Our survey revealed a few convinced Evangelicals who wear vestments (sometimes in one church in a team ministry) and adopt such practices as private confession, use of candles (especially

at baptism), the sign of the cross and 'extended'
Communion—all once regarded as very catholic.

In fact, the party issue in the Church of England is less
sharp now than at any time since the arrival of the Oxford
movement, except over the matter of women priests. As we
have seen, the evangelical wing is growing and the distinctively catholic wing is probably static or in slight decline. It
seems that more clergy wish to describe themselves as
'central', which means that they do not think of themselves
as members of a party, though quite a few then add 'evangelical' or 'catholic' to show their theological inclination.

THE BENCH OF BISHOPS

These shifts are also represented on the episcopal bench. In
1950 there was only one distinctively evangelical diocesan
bishop, and he presided over the miniscule diocese of Sodor
and Man. There was one suffragan—at Barking. It would
have been hard for Evangelicals then to imagine that early in
1980 both archbishoprics would be occupied by men of firmly
evangelical views (Blanch at York, Coggan at Canterbury) or
that half a dozen major dioceses would have evangelical
bishops. Even that number, of course, does not fairly represent
the size of the evangelical wing in the parishes—for that at
least eight or nine diocesans would be required. But it is not
unreasonable that the bench of bishops should predominantly
represent the centre stream of Anglican belief, provided its
members are genuinely sympathetic to the views and practices
of Evangelicals and Catholics. In any case it takes twenty or
thirty years for a shift of theological belief among new ordinands to be reflected in the episcopate.

In fact, the present bench of bishops is an impressive one—
far more impressive than most church people are inclined to
admit. It is an irritating Anglican trait to carp constantly
about the Church's leaders: few vicars seem to be enthusiastic
about their bishops, and nearly 30 per cent in our survey
described their relationship with the bishop as 'occasional',
'remote', 'unsympathetic' or 'non-existent'. But the view of
informed observers, especially in the media, is that the
Anglican bishops are, on the whole, good value—intelligent,

perceptive, articulate, scholarly and of broad sympathies. There are exceptions, some of them notorious, and too many have had little parochial experience, but as a bench they represent a formidable array of experience and talent: a scientist or two, several distinguished theologians, one or two philosophers, a couple of ethicists, several with a background in the media (three have been BBC producers), a former England cricket captain, a barrister, and three or four former missionaries. Most are still of public school and Oxbridge background, but slowly the number who were educated at State schools is increasing, and there are a few who did not go to university at all. Perhaps more importantly, most bishops nowadays do keep in touch with their clergy: over 70 per cent of clergy found their bishops to be close to them, 'supportive', 'encouraging' or 'understanding'. This is reflected in their public stance. When a bishop talks about bad housing in the inner city, racial tension or social strain through unemployment, he is speaking with knowledge. The clergy are *there*, probably more than any other professionals, actually living in the deprived areas and reporting accurately and sensitively to their bishops. The network is effective and efficient. At times it has seemed that some of the bishops have become the main spokesmen of the inarticulate, the public voice of the deprived.

Certainly they have made their mark in the media. It is true that in the past bishops have been columnists in the serious papers and have written important books. But it is, I think, unprecedented in Britain for bishops to be among the most popular broadcasters on the most popular radio stations, as Bill Westwood (Peterborough) and Jim Thompson (Stepney), for instance, have become on Radio 2. Perhaps we need to note their fashionably classless Christian names (shades of Hensley, Nicholas, Walsham and the rest). Their popularity does not rely on their saying popular things, but on their ability to relate to ordinary people: and their success is replicated in many parts of the country on local radio stations. Part of the price is a certain loss of supposed dignity, which seems a small price to pay, especially when it relies on such trivia as modes of address. Disc jockeys may not find 'my lord' a congenial addition to 'Mornin', mornin' ', but they demonstrably appreciate the willingness of a bishop to come across the old social barriers and become a friend to a predominantly lower-middle and working-class audience, where warmth and sincerity are more important than status.

What is true in broadcasting is true in the parish as well. Bishops are more approachable than they used to be. Instead of simply appearing once every other year or so for a confirmation service, they prefer to come more frequently on pastoral visits, perhaps spending a weekend in the parish, visiting some homes and small groups, talking to the youth fellowship, perhaps baptising some babies on Sunday morning and presiding at the eucharist. Increasingly ordinary lay people think of the bishop as 'their' bishop and are more aware of the Church as a national, and indeed international, body than they used to be. Parochialism is not dead, but it is not as rampant as it once was.

SYNOD

One reason for that, in my judgement, is the advent of synodical government. It has had its opponents and its detractors all along, and our survey shows that almost 36 per cent of clergy think that it has not benefited the Church. However, well over half (55 per cent) think that it *has*, and since part at least of its effect is to limit the rights of the bishops and clergy, that is quite a positive response.

From my observation it is not General Synod, which meets in London or York three times a year, that evokes most criticism, but its more local manifestations. The deanery synod is a rather pointless talking shop, whose sole useful executive function is to elect representatives to the diocesan (or area) synod. This, again, appears to be a rather nebulous body, which debates issues of current concern (General Synod is always relieved to decide of a thorny issue that it should be 'sent down to the dioceses') but has few real powers. However, its members elect General Synod, and there the true authority in the Church now lies. Synod holds the purse, and this gives it enormous power in the running of the Church's affairs.

But synod has done more than control the cash. It has also established itself as an important forum for debate. For centuries the General Assembly of the Church of Scotland has been recognised as a platform for the consideration of national as well as narrowly ecclesiastical matters. In England, there was no such tradition, though the old Church Assembly sometimes debated an issue such as capital punishment. But synod has proved an admirable forum and was quickly recognised by the media as a place where matters of conscience were intelligently but keenly debated.

Media interest has steadily increased, and very often the press and broadcasting facilities are over-stretched. Probably the greatest interest was in the synod's debate in 1984 on nuclear warfare, following publication of a report, *The Church and the Bomb*,[1] produced by a committee chaired by the Bishop of Salisbury. The report came down on the side of unilateral nuclear disarmament and was seized on by sections of the press and some politicians as evidence of the Anglican Church's leftward drift in politics.

Thus the subsequent synod debate was genuinely hot news. It was broadcast live on BBC radio and television and reported extensively in all the national newspapers. The result was probably a disappointment to the headline writers, though no surprise at all to experienced synod-watchers. By a comfortable majority, synod declined to support the report's unilateral stand, and opted instead for a multilateral alternative motion. Our survey of parochial clergy shows that synod accurately reflected their views.

The debate itself was brilliantly characterised by notable speeches on both sides, and conducted throughout without the point-scoring, bad temper or rudeness that often mars parliamentary occasions. There was passion, and arguments were genuinely confronted, but there was no bad feeling. It was a good day for the Church of England.

So undoubtedly was the debate on the bishops' statement on doctrine, in 1986, but some of the debates on the ordination of women have had the whiff of party strife about them—though not (as it happens) the one in 1987 that set the long procedural train in motion that may, one day, lead to the ordination of a woman to the Church's priesthood.

There have been many memorable moments in synod and

---

[1] Church House Publishing, 1984.

its predecessor, Church Assembly, often sad ones. Few who were there will ever forget Archbishop Michael Ramsey's response to the Assembly's failure to approve the scheme for Anglican–Methodist reunion to which he had lent all the weight of his office and his own considerable personal reputation as a churchman and a scholar. As he read out the voting figures, and it became clear that the necessary majority had not been reached in all three houses—of laity, clergy and bishops—some members began to applaud.

With that familiar hesitation of speech his voice cut across the applause. 'Silence would be more appropriate,' he commented. The clapping died away instantly.

I also remember the voting in synod on the Rite A alternative Communion service, with Colin Buchanan, a noted evangelical liturgical scholar, and Brian Brindley, a comparable figure from the catholic wing, combining time and again, with humour and sensitivity, to steer the entire service line by line through synod. If you want a monument to their achievement, look around you at the renewal of parish worship—but it was not achieved without hard work.

One of the most emotional moments in the synod's history came in 1986 when the Bishop of Durham rose to defend his position following the public controversy over his views on the Virgin Birth and the empty tomb. He knew that synod, and his fellow bishops, were overwhelmingly against his position and the way he had gone about publicising it. He knew that the motions before the house—motions that reaffirmed the very doctrines he had questioned—would be passed with large majorities.

He spoke as he always does, in a rush of words, phrases almost tumbling over each other. He was clearly under great strain, his faced flushed, his voice at times nearly breaking with emotion. It was a brilliant speech, brave to the point of foolhardiness; eloquent, passionate and arresting. It did not, in the event, win him votes, which went exactly as one had predicted they would. But it did win him respect, and even affection, from people who had come to denounce him as a heretic. The applause was long, warm and sincere. The Church of England had once again shown its traditional breadth of sympathy. There was to be no witch hunt. The

notorious 1987 debate on homosexuality was to reach much
the same conclusion.

Synodical government is by its nature government by
majority: majority, that is, of those eligible and able to vote.
It is a kind of diluted democracy, but for all that it has
involved lay people and parochial clergy in the Church's
decision making and opinion forming in a way that has never
happened in the Church of England before. Most of the
consequences are good. The one real disadvantage is that
radical or revolutionary ideas tend to be stifled—minorities
remain minorities, and the process of turning a minority view
into a majority one is obviously slow. The Church of Christ
has never been entirely 'democratic'. After all, it is, at heart,
a theocracy. Christ is the head of the body, no matter how
many votes are cast against him.

But the New Testament's two great images of the Church—
the family and the body—both presuppose the entire involvement of every member, and there is apostolic precedent for
the 'whole body of disciples' being part of the decision-making
process (Acts 6:2). Indeed, from early times even the election
of bishops was subject to popular approval.

ELECTION OF BISHOPS

It is here that synodical government has faced a daunting
task. How can a million lay members be involved, in any
effective way, in the decisions of the bishops, who to all
intents and purposes shape the life and ministry of the
Church? One answer is in their selection and election. So it
is not surprising that the election of bishops has been on or
close to the agenda of synod since it came into being.

Bishops were previously appointed by the sovereign, on the
advice of his or her Prime Minister, who was in turn advised
by an Ecclesiastical Appointments Secretary. That appointment was then approved by the dean and chapter of the
diocesan cathedral. Indeed, technically they 'elected' him, but
in practice it was rather like an election in Stalinist Russia—
there was only one candidate. It borders on the miraculous
that this system, which perpetuated some of the less admirable
features of the Holy Roman Empire of the late middle ages,

actually appointed such outstanding bishops as Hensley Henson, William Temple and Michael Ramsey.

But it *was* a bizarre system. Worse than that, it bordered on blasphemy, for the name of the Holy Spirit was invoked to guide in the election of a candidate chosen in fact by a political cabal. The emergence of synod brought a new system, introduced in the Callaghan administration, one which tried to balance what was seen as the appropriate involvement of the civil authorities of this 'Christian' nation with the Church's desire to set apart men chosen by the Holy Spirit (Acts 13:2).

The new system involved the creation of a national Crown Appointments Commission, chaired by an archbishop, and a local Vacancy in See Committee. There would be considerable consultation within and beyond the diocese, which would lead to the eventual submission by the Church of two names to the Prime Minister, a first choice and a second. Normally the Prime Minister would be expected to forward the first name to the sovereign, who would duly call upon the Church authorities to elect and install him as bishop. For the most part it seems to have worked well, with little evidence of the kind of political involvement in appointments that in the past saw Labour premiers appoint left-wing bishops and Tory ones those of conservative views. In fact, of course, it would be difficult (if not impossible) under this system for a Prime Minister to come up with a name not nominated by the church procedure.

Where difficulty has occurred (or is alleged to have occurred—obviously it is almost impossible to know the truth about such things), it has been where suspicions have arisen that the second and not the first choice has been sent to the sovereign. A notorious case came in the spring of 1987, with the appointment to the see of Birmingham. It is said that two names were submitted to the Prime Minister, those of the Bishops of Kensington and Stepney, and that Kensington was chosen (whether or not he was in fact first choice) because the Prime Minister had been led to believe that the Bishop of Stepney had socialist beliefs. Indeed, one backbench Tory MP claimed that he had personally intervened to warn the Prime Minister of the danger, and openly took the credit for frustrating what he saw as an undesirable appointment.

Of course, it may well be that protocol was meticulously followed and that the backbencher was claiming an influence he had never in fact had. Nevertheless the whole incident was both shocking and distasteful to church people. Newspapers ran stories about the 'banning' of a 'red bishop'. The two bishops involved were put in an impossible situation, and the Church was held up to ridicule—either for trying to elect a 'loony leftie' (if you took one view) or for giving in to secular political pressure (if you took the other). It is worth saying that whatever the rights and wrongs of the matter, neither of those propositions is remotely near the truth. The Bishop of Stepney is *not* a 'leftie', loony or otherwise, but a moderate, reforming bishop who has gone on record repeatedly about the bad effects of slum housing and unemployment in his area. For that matter, Bishop Mark Santer (then of Kensington) is no true-blue conservative either, but a publicly confessed pacifist and feminist. Nor did the Church bow to political pressure, because *both* the names were the Church's choice and would not have been put forward if it was not felt that they were both suitable for the see of Birmingham.

But damage was done, and that incident, and others like it, have strengthened the hand of those who demand change, including a few who want the State involvement in the appointment of bishops removed entirely. That is not likely to happen while the senior bishops have seats in the House of Lords—it would give the electors of the Church of England a quite unconstitutional role in the appointment of the government. However, if, as seems likely, the whole question of the composition of the House of Lords is one day examined, then the special place of the Church of England bishops in the government of the United Kingdom may well also be questioned, and the way be open to a method of appointment akin to other models where the State involvement is minimal and nominal—or even non-existent.

Arguments over episcopal appointments usually lead to someone writing to the *Daily Telegraph* to complain about 'all these trendy bishops'. 'Trendy' is itself an outmoded, sixties-style word, but it is still frequently attached (always as a term of abuse) to clergy who are thought to be compromising with current trends—hence, presumably, the sobriquet. In fact, as we have seen, the present trend in the Church is much as it is in society at large: towards a conservative set of values. The real 'trendies' nowadays would belong to the Prayer Book Society, long to bring back Evensong, and encourage children to learn the catechism and respect their elders and betters.

Of course there is always a danger of the Church simply imitating the world, picking up its latest buzz words ('enabler', 'mode', 'identification') and trying to christianise them. But there is almost certainly more danger of the Church retreating from the world, hiding itself in a comfortable, complacent ghetto isolated from the very things its founder regarded as of first importance: showing love to our neighbour, bearing one another's burdens, bringing good news to the poor. Time enough to worry about its image when the Church, like him, is accused of receiving sinners and eating with them.

CHAPTER SIX

THE ROMAN CATHOLIC CHURCH

THE STORY OF THE ROMAN CATHOLIC CHURCH in the British Isles since the Reformation is one of dogged survival, tenacious courage and eventual acceptance as a permanent and respected part of the religious landscape. Today the Church is dominant in the Republic of Ireland, militant in Northern Ireland, substantial in Scotland, growing in Wales and respectable in England. Over the whole of the United Kingdom, as our figures show, it has the largest committed membership of any denomination, though apart from pockets like Liverpool and Londonderry it still feels like a minority church in an alien culture. The Roman Catholic Church in Britain is still more defensive than its continental counterparts: possibly because of history, but more probably because the vast majority of its members are still today either immigrants themselves or are the children or grandchildren of immigrants. A glance at the list of clergy in the *Catholic Directory* is enough to prove the point: most of the surnames are of Irish origin.

Given the Church's history, this defensiveness is not very surprising. After all, until Catholic Emancipation in 1829 there were impenetrable barriers against the advance of Roman Catholics in British society. Go back not much more than a century before that, and one is in an era of physical persecution of catholicism characterised even by the execution of Roman Catholic priests. The horrors of the sixteenth century, with blood freely flowing both in the

Roman Catholic Churches, 1985

	Practising Adults*	Ministers	Churches†
England	1,377,144	4,385	3,024
Wales	146,673	200	324
Scotland	285,554	1,111	478
Northern Ireland	353,014	549	420
Totals	2,162,385	6,245	4,246

* Practising Adults = Mass attenders on average Sunday during the year.
† Figures for full number of church buildings and half of the other buildings open
  for Mass.

cause of the Reformation and against it, were slow to be forgotten, and the notion that all Roman Catholics were in fact traitors to the Crown of England survived into modern times (and is indeed still occasionally invoked today by militant Protestants).

Partly as a result of this, the Catholics were the last major group of Christians to take the ecumenical movement seriously. Understandably, they have theological as well as historic reasons for hesitation. 'Indifferentism', as it is known—the idea that all religions, or at any rate all versions of Christianity, lead to the same goal—is still a major stumbling block. If you claim to belong to the one true, holy, catholic and apostolic Church, and if you think that its principal distinctive is its relationship to the see of the first apostle Peter, then you cannot lightly accept the authenticity of other bodies that also claim to be part of that one true Church but are manifestly not in communion with the Bishop of Rome.

It was this, rather than any kind of bloody-mindedness, that kept the Roman Catholic Church out of the ecumenical scene for too long. Its priests were not permitted to take part in ecumenical events (except as observers), and its lay people were discouraged even from praying with non-Catholics. The British (and World) Council of Churches had only the most tenuous links with the world's largest Christian Church; and in most parts of the world, and especially in third-world mission fields, the prevailing mood was fierce competition rather than brotherly co-operation.

VATICAN II: REVERBERATIONS

The Second Vatican Council brought an enormous change. It tackled the ecumenical problem head on; it looked again at the standing of other ecclesiastical bodies, swallowed hard, and managed to call them 'Churches'. It dubbed Protestants and Orthodox 'separated brethren', and in phrases of transparent enthusiasm spoke of the divine calling to reunite the broken body of Christ. Without denying in the least way the unique place (as the Council saw it) of the Roman Catholic Church, it gave a warm signal of welcome to the other Churches: let us start to talk, let us start to act together, let us start to pray and even worship together.

The process was greatly helped, for Protestants at least, by other decisions of the Council, especially with regard to the Bible and worship. The work of the International Commission on English Texts, for instance, meant that many common parts of the liturgy—Creed, Gloria, Sanctus and so on—were in identical translations. Roman Catholic worship, which had seemed so foreign and remote, suddenly appeared to be familiar and friendly. Soon the new era of church music followed, which meant that Catholics and Protestants were also often singing the same songs in church. And when the hierarchy began to persuade Roman Catholic lay people to take an active role in inter-church activities, the change in temperature seemed complete.

But the theological differences remained, and it was inevitable that they would resurface. The temperature has warmed: there is no doubt about that. Catholics and Protestants respect each other, work together on matters of social concern, and locally often co-operate in house groups, Lent courses and even missions. Yet intercommunion, let alone actual church unity, seems farther away now than it did fifteen years ago. Liberal theology and women priests on the Protestant side, and a more intransigent traditional theology from a conservative Pope on the Roman Catholic side, have seen to that. There seems no likelihood of the Churches slipping back into the cold war of the past, but it requires stupendous optimism to see any serious moves towards church unity during the present pontificate.

However, ecumenism is not the great issue for the Roman

Catholic Church, though Pope John-Paul would undoubtedly welcome reunion with the Eastern Churches. In the West, including Britain, the Church has been preoccupied over the last two decades with other issues: holding the line against liberalism in ethical and theological matters, carrying through the reforms of the Second Vatican Council, halting the decline in active membership and encouraging a sufficient number of vocations to ensure an adequate supply of priests for the future. In the first area, the line *has* been held, but casualties have been heavy. In the second, after some initial misjudgements, the Council's principles have now permeated much of the life of the Church at parish level. In the third and fourth, the decline in attendance has slowed down; but the number of young men offering for ordination is still insufficient and the shortage of priests is creating problems in some dioceses.

Theological controversy has dogged the Church in the West for thirty years, strange as it may seem to those brought up on the idea that the Church of Rome is *semper eadem*, always the same. Substantial voices within the Church have questioned such fundamental things as its attitude to Scripture, its belief in papal infallibility, its doctrine of the priesthood, its veneration of Mary, even the Virgin Birth itself. On the ethical front its unequivocal condemnation of homosexuality, its stand against contraception and its attitude towards artificial insemination by a husband's sperm have all been rejected by some distinguished Catholic theologians.

The reaction of the hierarchy has changed since the early 1970s. At that time the approach of Cardinal Heenan, the Archbishop of Westminster, was probably typical. He suspended several teachers of theology—effectively taking away their authority to teach in Catholic institutions—for holding and propagating what he called 'liberal' views. There is no doubt that some *were* liberal, as anyone who has read Hubert Richards' books will recognise.[1] They challenged basic Catholic dogma and traditional Catholic practice, especially over priestly celibacy. In this period three or four extremely able theologians ceased to function as priests, among them John Harriott, editor of the Jesuit paper *The Month*; and

---

[1] eg Hubert John Richards, *The First Christmas: What really happened?* (Mowbray, 1983).

Adrian Hastings, who went on to teach theology at Leeds University. Both of them, as well as Richards and the writer Peter de Rosa, subsequently married. All still consider themselves to be practising Catholics, but their vast, if widely differing, talents are no longer available to the Church's ministry.

The reverberations of the encyclical *Humanae Vitae*, in which Pope Paul reaffirmed the Church's prohibition on all forms of artificial contraception, against the advice of his own appointed team of experts, continue to this day. Indeed, most married Roman Catholics in Western countries (other than Ireland, perhaps) do in fact use contraception, including the pill, and justify it on grounds often expounded by sympathetic parish priests: that an action is only sinful if it is taken against one's conscience. Hence those who can honestly say that their consciences are clear on this subject can (by this argument) practise artificial contraception without sinning. Sinning or not, most of them are clearly using contraception. Birth rates are much the same in Roman Catholic areas of England as they are in others. If the Church's rules were being scrupulously followed, that could not possibly be so.

Of course, having defied, or reinterpreted, or (a genuinely 'trendy' word!) *contextualised* the Church's teaching on contraception, and found that the sky had not fallen in, many Catholics have begun to pay less attention to a few other doctrines. The practice of private confession is both less widespread and less frequent than in the past; many Catholics prefer the idea of general absolution. This was introduced after Vatican II as an exceptional measure to draw lapsed communicants back to Mass, and was subsequently rather arbitrarily withdrawn in most dioceses when it proved too popular with ordinary parishioners. It had, after all, never been intended to replace the traditional Catholic practice of private confession.

Priestly celibacy has also been under a great deal of criticism, not only from the clergy, who in many cases might be the beneficiaries of any relaxing of the rules, but also from the laity, especially the core members. The first ever gathering of representative priests and lay people from parishes in England and Wales, the National Pastoral Congress held in Liverpool in 1980, expressed considerable disquiet about the effect of the celibacy rule, not only on the happiness and effectiveness of parish priests but also on the recruitment of ordinands. That priestly celibacy is not an unalterable principle has been demonstrated by the ordination to the priesthood of several married Anglican clergy who joined the Roman Catholic Church following the Durham controversy and the moves towards the ordination of women. In any case, it has always only been argued as a rule of the Church, not as a doctrine of the faith, and the presence for many centuries of married priests in some of the so-called uniate Churches in communion with Rome has made that clear. For that matter, St Peter himself, claimed to be the first Bishop of Rome, had a wife (1 Cor 9:5). No wonder some present-day priests, who long to be married, feel a sense of grievance; no wonder some men, once gifted priests and pastors but now barred from exercising a priestly office, feel that the Church is being irrationally unyielding on this point. Certainly marriage has robbed the English Church of several very gifted pastors and teachers, but the situation is far worse in several other European countries, notably Holland and West Germany.

Priestly celibacy was not the only issue over which that Pastoral Congress expressed views out of line with those of the present Pope. Intercommunion, or at any rate eucharistic hospitality, was also strongly supported. But the English bishops, while probably for the most part sympathising with those views, held back from publicly endorsing them, which would have put them on a collision course with the Pope himself. Instead, the whole operation was shunted into a siding, where it has remained ever since. The delegates to the Congress dubbed themselves 'the Easter People', but the harsh truth is that the expected new dawn of English catholicism simply failed to lift itself above the horizon.

It cannot, however, be denied that the Roman Catholic Church in Britain is in good heart. Its day-to-day life of worship and witness is not marked by disputes, and there is little sense of grievance or anxiety among the majority of its active lay people. They are, mostly, well aware how much better their situation is post-Vatican II. The leadership of the Church, taken collectively, is not very colourful, but the visit of Pope John-Paul in 1982 had a marvellous effect on morale,

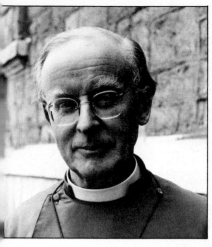

Donald Coggan, Archbishop of Canterbury 1974–1980 — during a period when the Church of England began to recover its nerve. See page 58.

Photo: Keith Ellis

chard Harries, broadcaster, writer
d Bishop of Oxford: a formative
luence in the Church of England.

oto: Keith Ellis

Una Kroll, doctor, deacon, one of the first to argue in public the rights of women in the Church of England.

Photo: Keith Ellis

Archbishop of Canterbury during a turbulent period for the Church: Dr Robert Runcie.

Photo: Keith Ellis

Cardinal Basil Hume, Benedictine monk and Archbishop of Westminster, widely admired but a low profile leader.
See page 98.

Photo: Keith Ellis

Archbishop Derek Worlock and Bishop David Sheppard
lay a foundation stone on a Toxteth building site.

Photo: Mercury Press Agency Ltd

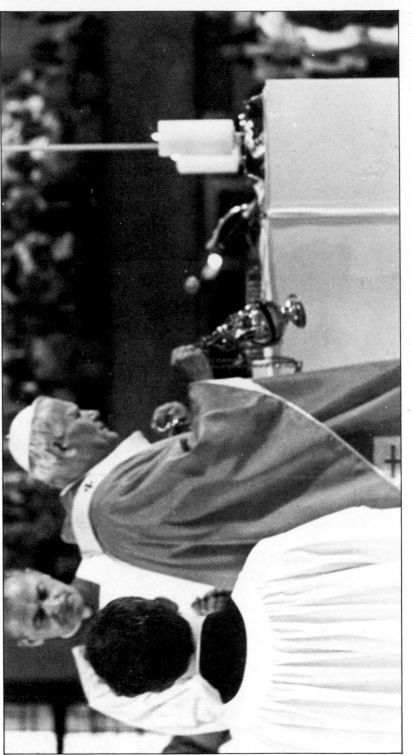

Pope John Paul celebrates Mass in the Metropolitan Cathedral, May 1982.

Kenneth Slack, one of the major Free Church figures of the seventies and eighties, but finally best known as an outstanding broadcaster. See Chapter 7.

Photo: Keith Ellis

...uline Webb, missionary and ...umenical diplomat, ...oadcaster and writer — one ...the most influential figures the Free Churches.

...oto: Keith Ellis

'A high pressure, fizzy kind of religious experience': the Spring Harvest participants face the BBC television cameras for *Songs of Praise*. See page 119.

'There is now a much broader consensus on the importance of "mission"'. One of its strongest advocates is Gavin Reid, author, clergyman, evangelist. See page 52.

Photo: Church of England Newspaper

'The charismatic movement has taught leaders and
congregations about body-language, about feeling as well
as saying, about enthusiasm as well as order.' See Chapter 9.

Photo: Church of England Newspaper

The annual Greenbelt Festival — 25,000 young men and
women prove that Christianity is not a lost cause with the
new generation. See page 31.

Photo: Church of England Newspaper

and in reminding British Catholics of the world-wide nature of their Church. The Roman Catholic Church is a strong, coherent body, still able to speak out on major issues with one voice, still able to evoke an impressive loyalty from its members. That, incidentally, is why any ecumenical advance without it is hardly worthy of the name.

My impression of the Church on mainland Britain is created by a number of abiding images. There is the Pope, of course: a small, white dot in the distance in human terms as he preached and said Mass in one massive stadium or amphitheatre after another, yet for the vast crowds of worshippers an intense focal point of loyalty and commitment. Few non-Catholics would have agreed with everything he said, but many would have envied the authority with which he spoke it and the reverence—approaching awe—with which such enormous numbers of people received it. There was exuberance and joy, too, capturing some of the spirit of *aggiornamento* (renewal) that Pope John XXIII brought to the Church when he flung open the windows of the Vatican and let the air in.

The crowds sang: mostly songs like 'Our God Reigns', which became the papal signature tune. But occasionally, as at Coventry, one of the old Catholic hymns would be heard— 'Soul of my Saviour'—evoking in many a convent-educated woman a tear of nostalgia for the former times, when nuns dressed like nuns, incense shrouded the altar, and the Mass was in Latin. The mixture is formidable, compounded of intense juvenile devotion, early indoctrination and the intangible influences of sights, sounds and smells from the past. There is something uniquely poignant about a lapsed Catholic, as Graham Greene knew. And some *have* lapsed, especially in England. Often the rules over birth control are the difficulty, but more often it is simply the pull of an unsympathetic partner, or ordinary materialism that edges people away from the Church. Some do come back; a few end up in one of the other denominations, usually in the Anglican Church; but hardly any can shake off entirely the effects of a Catholic upbringing or schooling.

This is another image: of a primary school Mass in a Roman Catholic school in the East End of London. The children had prepared much of the service—chosen the songs,

rehearsed the readings, written out their prayers for the intercessions. They acted as servers and stewards. A little boy and
a little girl, one white and the other black, brought up the
bread and wine at the offertory. Almost all the children
received Communion. It was a transparently happy and good
occasion, but its most distinctive mark was the reverence of
the children—I can think of no other word, though that one
is quite inadequate to capture the wide-eyed wonder, the
simple, untroubled faith and the innocent joy of the young
communicants. One trembled for their future, for the world
is not like this. Indeed, even the Church is not often like this.
But they were receiving something more precious than mere
memories and sensations, something literally priceless. I hope
they will one day realise how privileged they were.

A third image is of the episcopal ordination of a friend and
former colleague in a Midlands cathedral. It was an obviously
and distinctly catholic occasion, the contrast being underlined
for me because it was within a day or two of the consecration
of another friend as an Anglican bishop. The service was very
long, well over two hours. The music was mostly modern,
very well sung, both by choir and congregation. The homily,
by Cardinal Hume, was typically folksy and exactly right for
the occasion. I found the Litany of the Saints surprisingly
moving. I suppose it was the effect of being in a vast crowd
of people who genuinely felt the presence with us of all these
marvellous men and women of the past: St Widesfrid, for
instance, or my own personal favourite, St Ambrose of Milan.
It was as though (as Cardinal Hume put it) they were
crowding around us to see what the new bishop was like.

Yet the really memorable thing about the occasion, for me
at least, was the congregation itself: quite unlike the one at
the Anglican occasion, which was definitely well-heeled and
discreet. My pew, which was seriously overcrowded, was
largely occupied by nuns and friends from their parishes. The
long wait before the service was an opportunity for
unashamed gossip, into which I was irresistibly drawn. There
was much merriment and warmth (and it was a hot day, too).
During the service, however, there was a sense of involvement,
both human and spiritual, if one may make the distinction.
There were occasionally whispered comments ('Who's the
very tall bishop?' 'I know the reader, he's from the next

parish') but there was also an almost intense desire to be involved. Having earlier established that I was an Anglican approaching my own ordination, the nun next to me leant over (though there was hardly need to) to whisper, 'I'll pray for you at the altar.' At the moment of consecration, her eyes fixed on the elevated Host, she uttered to herself with surprising emphasis the words of doubting Thomas: 'My *Lord* and my *God!*'

I know none of this is very unusual or novel. In its context, however, it reminded me that the roots of English catholicism are in the culture of ordinary working people, whatever their distant racial origins, and that both loyalty to the group and generosity to those outside it are part of that heritage, at its best. My friend, who comes from an English middle-class background, was duly ordained. 'He looks a lovely man,' said my neighbour, 'God bless him.'

English catholicism is rather different from that of Scotland and Northern Ireland, a fact which occasionally eludes London-based commentators. Indeed, Liverpool catholicism is also unlike that of the Midlands or the South, partly because of a history of sectarian strife in the city, partly because of sheer numbers. The last decade in Liverpool has seen a quite remarkable change of atmosphere, largely brought about by the efforts of the Roman Catholic archbishop, Derek Worlock, and the Anglican bishop, David Sheppard. A city once scarred by religious bitterness and bigotry has become a sign of what can be done when wise leaders are prepared to take calculated risks.

The Roman Catholic Church in Scotland pursues its own way, very dominant in some areas (Glasgow, and some islands) and enjoying, if that is the right word, a slightly tentative relationship with the majority Church of Scotland. It looks with paternal concern across the Irish Sea to its sister Church in Northern Ireland; the concern is not entirely unselfish, for part of it is concern lest the troubles of Ulster should seed themselves back to similar soil in parts of Scotland.

The Northern Ireland situation is unique. Its solution calls for a largeness of heart and breadth of vision which has so far eluded the leaders of both the Roman Catholic and the Protestant Churches. It is true that most leaders of both religious communities are unequivocal and even eloquent in their denunciations of violence. But it is equally true that when the real moments of decision come, they tend to revert to tribal loyalties. Dr Paisley is a menace, senior Protestant church leaders will tell you: 'but mind you, there's a lot of truth in what he says.' The 'men of violence' (code language for the Provisional IRA) are cold-blooded murderers, say responsible Catholic clerics: 'but you must see it all against a background of centuries of injustice and discrimination.' One day there may arise a leadership in Ulster, on both sides, that eschews the tragic conjunction 'but'. Until that happens, good Christian people, who long for nothing more than to live in peace with their neighbours, will be endlessly disappointed.

One group that has transcended this sectarian divide in Ulster is the charismatic movement, which is probably stronger on the Catholic than the Protestant side. Ecumenical prayer groups exist, and indeed flourish, though they are wisely unpublicised. Much more publicised are ventures like Corrymeela, the interdenominational centre for reconciliation, where (mainly) youngsters from both communities learn to work and worship together. Of course Corrymeela is a sign of hope, but it is a small island of peace in a large and troubled sea. Its vision is worth nourishing, but (that word again) it would need a revolution in attitudes for it to be widely shared. That is why I would have rather more hope in the charismatic movement: the Holy Spirit has a way of changing attitudes from within. That is where the revolution must begin.

Sadly, many English Protestants tend to judge Roman Catholicism by what they see, hear and read about Northern Ireland. Oddly, they do not similarly judge Protestantism. English Roman Catholics, on the other hand, are well aware that Ian Paisley does not represent the sort of Christian they meet in their local Baptist or Methodist Church.

The Roman Catholic Church will probably continue to have a love-hate relationship with the British people. Today there is little antagonism towards it, but many people do not consider it as a religious option: it is simply not a Church towards which they feel temperamentally drawn. That probably explains the very low number of actual conversions to Roman Catholicism in England and Wales. Those who are seeking God tend to seek him in a more familiar environment. While it is true that the Church of England, for instance, has seldom had a mass appeal for the working classes, it is equally true that the Roman Communion, for whatever reason, has seldom had any appeal at all for the native-born English. If Britain is ever to return to communion with the see of Rome, it must surely be through some new relationship between the Roman Catholic Church and the great indigenous Churches of Britain, whether Presbyterian or episcopal.

That may well happen, but the date has unquestionably been set back by recent events. Many Anglicans have few difficulties over accepting some kind of international primacy for the Bishop of Rome, but they cannot expect to bring with them into a united Church (or even into some relationship of intercommunion along uniate lines) the theology of the Bishop of Durham or the practice of ordaining women to the priesthood. So the matter will have to rest, either until Rome changes its mind on women priests (and liberal theology) or until Protestants are prepared to swallow a great deal more than they appear to be prepared to swallow at present.

Until then, the Roman Catholic Church in Britain will continue to witness to its claim to be the only fully legitimate expression of apostolic Christianity. It will do it, as it has done for the last couple of decades, with courtesy and restraint, but that should not blind others to the nature of its claim. In changing circumstances, some might find that claim irrefutable and submit their allegiance to Rome. Others will continue to resist it and only enter into communion on terms approaching parity. That is the nub of the ecumenical dilemma.

Meanwhile, Britain's five million or so Roman Catholics will remain loyal to the Pope and their Church (as will the equal number not recorded as 'practising': the total of four million is almost a tenth of the adult population). The noisy rebellion against the liturgical changes of the Council (particularly the virtual disappearance of the Tridentine Mass) has all but died out. A mere handful continue the campaign, but they know that it is a lost cause. The 'new' Church, with its vernacular liturgy, its lay ministry, its emphasis on involvement rather than adherence, has weathered a difficult period and is about to enter calmer waters. It would be nice to think

that in more peaceful surroundings it might be more inclined
to signal to its partners in the other boats.

CHAPTER SEVEN

THE FREE CHURCHES

EOPLE WHO SEE VAST NINETEENTH-CENTURY
chapels turned into warehouses assume that the great
Free Church tradition they represent has been taken
over by other causes. Of course the Free Churches
have shared in the general decline in regular churchgoing,
but not more so than the other denominations (and less
so, probably, than the Church of England). They are still a
substantial presence in the religious life of Britain in their
three main presentations: Methodist, Presbyterian[1] and Baptist. They have produced a disproportionately large number
of distinguished figures in the arts, politics and journalism,
and the nonconformist conscience is still an influential element
in decision-making in Britain. So 'fast-fading dissent', as it
has been dubbed, is a gross exaggeration.

Methodist Churches, 1985

	Members	Ministers	Churches
England	424,851	3,372	7,117
Wales	22,561	193	415
Scotland	7,008	34	73
Northern Ireland	20,792	244	126
Totals	475,212	3,843	7,731

[1] I shall, of course, exclude the Church of Scotland from this chapter because,
although its doctrine and order are firmly in the Free Church tradition, it is not
nonconformist, but is the established Church of its nation, and therefore distinctly
different in ethos from other Free Churches.

Presbyterian Churches, 1985

	Members*	Ministers	Churches
England	127,197	1,325	1,790
Wales	84,750	268	1,212
Scotland	901,914	1,513	2,142
Northern Ireland	274,737	532	595
Totals	1,388,598	3,638	5,739

* These figures include the United Reformed Church in England.

Baptist Churches, 1985

	Members	Ministers	Churches
England	164,243	1,869	2,310
Wales	45,611	245	785
Scotland	17,666	175	190
Northern Ireland	8,000	70	85
Totals	235,520*	2,359	3,370

* These figures include non-Union churches listed in the *Baptist Union of Great Britain & Ireland Directory*.

Free Churches, 1985 (excluding Scotland)

	Members	Ministers	Churches
Baptist, Methodist & Presbyterian	1,162,742	8,118	14,435
Independents	268,957	2,176	4,441
Totals	1,431,699	10,294	18,876

THE METHODISTS

Comfortably the largest of these churches is the Methodist Church, very strong in parts of England (Devon, Cornwall and the North-East, for instance), with about half a million members. As we have seen, it was the product, or perhaps the by-product, of the Wesleyan revival, at first a movement within and subsequently a division from the Anglican Church. Methodism itself then split into several groupings, initially on the issue of 'election'—John Wesley himself took the Arminian view (broadly, that we contribute at least our own response to God's calling), while many Methodists, following George Whitefield, took a Calvinistic view (broadly, that we contribute absolutely nothing to our own salvation, not even our response to God's call). Hence, until this century (and still today, in Wales and a few other places) there were Wesleyan Methodists and Calvinist Methodists, their chapels sometimes built on adjoining sites, and their members stubbornly disowning their fellow Methodists next door. Other, more obscure, differences also divided Methodism: over church order, the sacraments, revivalism and lay ministry. It was 1932 before most (though not all) of the divisions were healed.

A considerable liberal movement in Methodist theology probably contributed more to the eventual reunion of Methodism than any sudden outbreak of charity. After all, Christians who are unsure about the inspiration of Scripture, the possibility of miracles or (even) the divinity of Christ are hardly likely to separate over arcane issues of church order. Liberalism became the predominant flavour of Methodist theology in the 1920s and 1930s, and still today I suspect that only a minority of Methodist ministers unreservedly share John Wesley's views on Scripture and salvation. There is much talk in Methodist circles of hearts being 'strangely warmed', but the experience is not, generally, based on the Augustinian and Lutheran doctrine of justification that John Wesley espoused. But the concept of freely available grace is still a prevalent theme in Methodism, giving to its worship and spirituality a freedom and sense of gratitude that is genuinely contagious.

Most Methodists, in my experience, are really 'liberal evangelicals', which I suppose is shorthand for those who adopt the perspective I have just described. The Church was born out of an evangelical revival and, to a lesser extent, out of its Calvinistic reflection. It kept the fervour, but after a hundred years of doctrinal disputes it has tended to turn its back on dogma. Methodist theologians have been in the forefront of speculative theology, of ecumenical experiment, of inter-faith dialogue and the application of Christian principles to matters of social and political concern. Plenty of boats have been rocked and sacred cows slaughtered without disrupting the

denomination. Some ministers have been charged with
heresy—Donald Soper, for one—but that was nearly fifty
years ago, and the allegations did not prevent his election
twenty-five years later as President of the Methodist Conference. On the whole, Methodists have cultivated an inclusivist
theology, which can encompass without too much stress the
three main emphases in the denomination: liberalism, evangelicalism, and catholicism.

The majority of liberally minded ministers and lay people
accept that their Church also includes Radicals, Evangelicals
and Catholics. The Radicals (banding together under ARM—
the Association of Radical Methodists) are contemptuous
of traditional Church order and dogma. For them, the old
institution must die, or be destroyed, in order to give way to
a new People's Church, a phoenix arising from the ashes of
the old Christendom. Their vision is of a Church engaged
with the 'world' at every level, creating base communities on
the Latin American pattern, working for individual and social
liberation. Many of the radical Methodists are highly politi-
cised and deeply involved in CND, COPEC (Christian Organisations for Social, Political and Economic Change), CARAF
(Christians Against Racism and Fascism), ELSA (End Loans
to South Africa) and similar causes. Probably their best known
exponent is John Vincent, leader of the Urban Theology
Project based in Sheffield.

The Radicals are a small but prominent group of activists.
So, in a quite different way, are the conservative Evangelicals.
They are undoubtedly a growing force in Methodism. Their
best-known figure is probably Donald English, President of
Conference in 1978/9 and a prominent supporter of Billy
Graham. Their movement went under the slightly misleading
title of the Methodist Revival Fellowship until it joined up
with Conservative Evangelicals in Methodism under the new
title of Headway. This group has several thousand lay and
ministerial members—though evangelicalism in the
Methodist Church stretches a good deal further than Headway's membership. Cliff College, in Derbyshire, has traditionally trained many young lay Methodists for ministry with an
evangelical ethos, and Methodists have also been fairly widely
involved in such evangelical organisations as the Universities
and Colleges Christian Fellowship (formerly Inter-Varsity

Fellowship), Scripture Union and the Evangelical Alliance. In recent years a fairly strong charismatic group has emerged in Methodism, with a magazine called *Dunamis*.

The catholic movement in Methodism is also small, and probably less prominent—certainly less strident—than the Radicals or Evangelicals. It gathers itself around the Methodist Sacramental Fellowship, and believes that it is faithful to the high sacramentalism of much of the Wesley brothers' theology. With that theology, its supporters have introduced into Methodist Churches such practices as the wearing of stoles, the use of confession, the sign of the cross, veneration of the Virgin Mary and the saints—and even the use of the rosary! Its best-known figures are undoubtedly Neville Ward—whose books echo a thoroughly catholic spirituality—and Gordon Wakefield. Traditional Methodists regard these Weslo-Catholics with the same benign tolerance as they do the Radicals and the Evangelicals: all part of the rich fabric of a truly 'free' Church.

For all its ecumenism, Methodism is a highly 'denominational' Church, as even a casual reading of the *Methodist Recorder* will reveal. Its structure and organisation, laid down by John Wesley himself, are unique in Christendom. Its ministers used to be moved about by Conference, for all the world like Jesuits at the command of the Vicar General, or Salvationists at the word of the High Command. The 'class' system, the society stewards, the famous preaching plan (which ensures that Methodist preachers tour their circuit like travelling salesmen)—all of these are totally distinctive to Methodism. The amazing thing is not that so distinctive a system of church order and ministry could survive 200 years, but that it actually seems to work quite well. The Methodists have much to offer a future united Church, provided anyone can be found to unite with them.

THE SALVATION ARMY

The Salvation Army had early links with Methodism but can now be regarded as a denomination, though it has no sacraments as such. With about 60,000 members it is a highly visible part of British Christianity, best known for its social work—hostels, medical centres, old people's homes and so on—and for its brass bands. There is probably no Christian Church more uniformly well regarded by the general public, but the Army is not more notably successful than the other churches in reaching the outsider with the gospel, for all its multifarious contacts. It may be that the rather quaint uniform and generally authoritarian air of the movement deters some people from joining. The present General, Eva Burrows, and many of the new breed of leaders are, I think, well aware of the problem and of ways in which things could be changed.

THE PRESBYTERIANS

The Presbyterian tradition in Britain is most strongly represented in Northern Ireland and Scotland, where it is the predominant flavour of Protestantism. It is also quite strong in Wales, but—largely for historical reasons—it is a relatively small element in English church life. Most of the former Presbyterian Churches in England had a strong Scottish or Irish flavour, but they were willing to be absorbed into the United Reformed Church, in what has generally proved a happy marriage with the English Congregationalists. The new Church is not a large one, but it is in many ways a genuine 'bridge' Church. It is an instance of the independent and Presbyterian forms of church order successfully merging into a pattern of government that combines elements of both, with a good deal of local freedom.

Still, it was all too much for some Congregationalists, whose commitment to the autonomy of the local church completely ruled out such notions as district moderators. It was all too 'connexial', too 'denominational' for them, and so several small continuing congregationalist groups stayed out of the new body and show no sign of withering away.

As in the case of the Methodists, the prevailing theological flavour of the United Reformed Church is liberal, though it has a small evangelical group (known by the acronym GEAR) and has not been entirely impervious to the charismatic movement. Nevertheless, its members' main concerns seem to be the application of Christian principles to socio-political issues; its ministers are prominent in various pressure groups (on the environment, peace, nuclear energy and so on), and its excellent magazine *Reform* devotes much space to similar ethical issues. Much of the denomination's strength is in rural areas; but this means that many churches have a small membership, and survival is often the first item on the agenda. Sadly, the fifteen years of the URC have seen a steady fall in membership—as is also true of most of the groups that stayed out of the merger. By the end of 1987 their combined membership was under 140,000.

From its birth the URC has seen itself as a pilot plant for ecumenical experiment. Its second moderator, John Huxtable, was an eloquent advocate of a covenant scheme in the seventies, which was intended to break the ecclesiastical log-jam and get *all* the Churches of England moving towards eventual unity along the path of an interim commitment to an eventual goal (hence the 'covenant'). In fact, the project foundered on the almost inevitable problems involved in uniting Churches of catholic order with those of a liberal protestant tradition. Many charitable words were spoken, but the Baptists were never very enthusiastic about it, and when the Church of England synod failed to give the covenant scheme sufficient backing, it joined a generous file of failed unity schemes in the ecumenical archives.

THE BAPTISTS

The Baptists—a title that covers a wide variety of churches—are a substantial element in British Christianity. Some churches which have the name 'Baptist' in their title have nothing whatever to do with the Baptist Union, but are in effect independent evangelical churches who practice believers' baptism. It is hard to assess the real strength of the Baptist cause, since even the Baptist Union is a very loose association of independent churches rather than a Church in any denominational sense. But my impression is that across the United Kingdom the Baptists (interpreting the title broadly) are a growing force, benefiting from the general upsurge in evangelicalism and providing the main and often sole link between the traditional churches and the House Church movement, much of which is Baptist in theology.

Although there is a liberal element within the Baptist Union (which is why many evangelical congregations refuse to be associated with it) the whole denomination is probably more evangelical now than at any time this century. Baptists have taken a prominent role in inter-Church affairs since the war, with men like Ernest Payne, Edwin Robertson and David Russell prominent and respected across the world; but in recent years they have tended to back off from the ecumenical scene, largely under pressure from their evangelical wing. Their world-wide links are, however, very strong.

Baptists are the largest grouping of Protestants internationally, and are especially strong in the United States, so that they are more open than other churches to American influence. Hence Baptist churches have given the lead in appointing musical directors, developing new-style Sunday schools and using their church plant in creative ways. Giving is relatively high among British Baptists (tithing is fairly common) and they support a disproportionately high number of missionaries and other full-time workers.

The charismatic movement has profoundly influenced many Baptist churches. Many of their young people and families attend conventions like Spring Harvest, where they learn some new songs and perhaps some 'original' ideas, especially about the nature of worship. It is often from these sources that new practices are introduced. In recent years, for instance, many Baptist churches, and others, have taken to incorporating long sequences of worship songs in their services, with the expectation that they will then experience the Lord 'inhabiting the praises of his people'—a rather odd interpretation of Psalm 22:3, based on a mistranslation in the King James Version. The rationale of this practice is that in this experience of musical worship Jesus will become present 'in a special way', though *how* this presence is more special than that promised by him ('where two or three come together in my name, there am I with them') is not at all clear.

Of course, this practice is by no means widespread in Baptist churches. Indeed, many stick pretty rigidly to the time-honoured hymn sandwich, with the minister not only leading the service and preaching but also doing all the praying— and even sometimes the reading of Scripture—himself. While being more committed in theory to the priesthood of all believers than, say, the Anglicans, there remains a type of Free Church minister who has made one-man ministry into an art form.

Somewhere between the neo-charismatic and the die-hard conservative one can find a third kind of Baptist congregation, probably by now the majority. Here the leading of worship is shared by minister and lay people (men and women); the music is a mixture of old and new; and the congregation is encouraged to participate in the prayers, sometimes by the use of responses, sometimes by encouraging members to lead the whole congregation in prayer—usually extempore.

None of these forms of worship is unique to Baptists, of course. What *is* distinct is the practice of believers' baptism. In contrast to the almost universal practice of Christendom from the immediate post-apostolic period to the Reformation, Baptists restrict baptism to adults who profess faith, and the rite itself is usually by total immersion. This has several important consequences. It emphasises *membership*, as distinct from adherence. It keeps faith (and the content of that faith) absolutely central in the Church's thinking. It makes an experience of conversion, and the willingness to testify to it, the essential element in Christian initiation. Logically, the children of Baptist parents are the objects of evangelism, rather than discipleship, and this tends to determine the church's programme and strategy towards youth work.

But it has also helped it keep Baptist theology evangelical, or at any rate evangelistic. Of all the major denominations, it is the Baptists who are most nearly an evangelical church. Even the more liberal Baptists—churches like Bloomsbury, in London, which have a long-standing liberal tradition— preach for conversion. Indeed, it is hard to see how they could do otherwise, given a commitment to believers' baptism.

With that emphasis goes a more thorough-going Protestantism where the other gospel sacrament is concerned. Baptists in general hold a Zwinglian view of the Lord's supper: that is, it is a memorial, rather than a sacrifice, sacrament or means of grace. They 'remember the Lord in the breaking of bread'. The 'real presence' is associated with the once-for-all experience of conversion and (for those of a charismatic inclination) the experience of common worship—not with a sacrament. Consequently Holy Communion is still usually celebrated as a postscript to one of the regular worship services, rather than as a separate ordinance. Individual communion cups—common in all the Free Churches—may have been introduced primarily for reasons of hygiene, but they do in fact also symbolise the idea of a personal experience of Christ personally commemorated. In fact, it is this personal faith that is the hallmark of Baptist spirituality, shaping not only its view of salvation, but also of Church order and doctrine. Baptist Churches are notoriously unenthusiastic about centralisation, whether in organisation or doctrine, though they are happy to 'associate together' with other Churches in the Union in terms of fellowship. But each local church, is, theologically speaking, its own Vatican, making its own rules and order, and jealous of this independence whenever it is threatened.

In recent years a number of Anglican Evangelicals have looked rather enviously at the Baptist practice of believers' baptism, and some clergy have virtually adopted it, in fact if not in theory. There has, in any case, been a move towards adult baptism in all the Churches, largely because fewer babies are baptised nowadays. Sometimes this takes the form of total immersion. However, Baptists are less inclined now than they were a century ago to insist on total immersion as the only valid form of baptism. I remember one distinguished Baptist minister pointing out to a meeting many years ago that they accepted a token amount of bread and wine in the Lord's Supper, could they not reasonably accept also a token amount of water in baptism? However, there is a great attachment to the symbolism of immersion, especially the notion of burial and resurrection, and it seems likely to remain the normal and distinctive Baptist practice for the foreseeable future.

FREE CHURCH UNITY

The English Free Churches have expressed their common inheritance by mutual intercommunion and, to a large extent, interchange of ministers. It is not uncommon for a minister to serve at different times in Baptist, Reformed and Methodist churches. Dr Leslie Weatherhead, a distinguished Methodist, was for many years minister of the (then Congregationalist)

City Temple in London. There is a good deal of joint theological training, easy transference of lay membership, and many joint churches—quite a few including Baptists (though their problems of co-operation are obviously more difficult).

The outward expression of this Free Church unity is the Free Church Federal Council, to which all the major Free Churches belong. Its moderator, elected annually, is regarded as the country's senior Free Churchman, at any rate on formal occasions. Recent occupants of the post have indeed been outstanding ministers—Dr Kenneth Slack (URC), for instance, and Dr Donald English (Methodist)—and have achieved, in their brief moderatorship, a degree of national recognition. But a year is a very short time in church affairs, and it is a sad truth that the media, for instance, cannot understand why a man who is a leader today is back in the ranks tomorrow. Archbishops, bishops and cardinals they can understand: these are distinctive roles, and their occupants tend to be around for a long while. But moderators, especially moderators who only last for twelve months, are hard to come to terms with. This simple fact, more than any prejudice against nonconformity, probably accounts for the rather poor media coverage of Free Church beliefs and opinion.

However, there is no shortage of distinguished Free Churchmen in public life: Lord Tonypandy, who as George Thomas was for many years Speaker of the House of Commons, is well known as a Methodist preacher and leader. Economist Sir Fred Catherwood; Labour foreign affairs spokesman Donald Anderson; life peer Lord Soper; and BBC Controller, Northern Ireland, Colin Morris are all distinguished Free Churchmen. And two of Britain's last three Prime Ministers—Harold Wilson and Margaret Thatcher— were born in the Free Church tradition. The list could easily be extended across every area of life in Britain.

The nonconformist conscience has helped to create democracy and social concern in British political life. Some argue that it gave birth to the Labour Party. It certainly helped to form a public consensus about freedom, justice and responsibility over the vital decades in which modern Britain shaped itself—broadly, the Victorian and Edwardian eras. Today its influence is less overt, but it is still there. Free Churches are often in the forefront of local pressure groups; their ministers still often take up unpopular social causes; their members are often active in housing associations, community groups, schemes for the unemployed and self-help projects.

The Free Churches are far from dead. The Methodists have recently seen a slowing-down in the numerical decline they had been suffering for many decades—from over 600,000 members in 1970 to just over 450,000 in 1987. The Baptists have done better, and have actually seen their numbers rise in the 1980s. They have made better use of women in leadership and ministry than the other Churches, and have reaped the benefit. The fifteen denominations who form the Free Church Federal Council had a membership at the end of 1987 of almost three-quarters of a million: that is still a powerful and influential grouping in British society. A further three-quarters of a million outside the Council further augment the Free Church influence.

The tradition that has produced in my lifetime a theologian of the calibre of C H Dodd, a church statesman of the stature of Lesslie Newbigin, a social reformer of the quality of Kenneth Greet and a preacher as redoubtable as W E Sangster, cannot be dismissed lightly. And these are just names picked at random; one could add during the same period Baptists like the late Stephen Winward, and Paul Beasley-Murray; Methodists like John Newton and Gordon Rupp; and URC ministers like Philip Morgan and Gordon Wakefield. All the signs are that the worst period of numerical decline is now in the past. A bright future for the Free Churches may well provide a similar wealth of talent, wisdom and leadership for the Church of the next century.

CHAPTER EIGHT

THE EVANGELICALS

As I have surveyed the different church traditions in Britain I have had occasion to note the evangelical groups or movements within them. Evangelicals are a growing force in the Church of England and the Church in Wales, and are present in substantial numbers in the Baptist, Methodist and United Reformed/Presbyterian Churches, especially in Northern Ireland. In this chapter, however, I want to look at evangelicalism from a different perspective: as a movement in its own right, a distinct if amorphous grouping of churches and individuals across all kinds of denominational labels and loyalties.

The movement presents itself in various public guises. The Evangelical Alliance claims to speak for 'a million Evangelicals', though its actual membership, of individuals and churches, is no more than a fraction of that. The British Evangelical Council, historically a sternly reformed body, links together several hundred independent evangelical churches, many very small but some—like Westminster Chapel in London—very large. Scripture Union, the UCCF (Universities and Colleges Christian Fellowship, formerly the Inter-Varsity Fellowship), London Bible College, the Christian Literature Crusade, TEAR Fund (for famine relief), the Overseas Missionary Fellowship, the Keswick Convention 'for the deepening of the spiritual life' and youth movements like Crusaders and Covenanters are typical of the umbrellas under which Evangelicals meet and co-operate. Many Evangelicals pay little attention to denominational membership: to find a 'keen' or 'sound' church is more important than loyalty to an ecclesiastical tradition. Consequently evangelical congregations frequently include a bewildering mixture of church backgrounds, with some members having been baptised as babies (ex-Anglicans perhaps) and others never having been baptised at all (ex-Salvation Army).

The great interdenominational institutions of evangelicalism are not the force they once were—the change of stance of Anglican Evangelicals has been an important factor here—but they are still major rallying points. Time was when their 'May meetings' in London filled the Central Hall or even the Royal Albert Hall. Now their ambitions are more modest, but the various residential conferences and conventions are probably better attended than in the past (Spring Harvest attracts some 50,000 people to three weeks of intensive Bible study, worship and seminars) and the traditional evangelical propensity for meetings and fellowships guarantees plenty of opportunities for people to belong to office, works, college or school evangelical groups.

The UCCF has played a powerful role in shaping evangelical belief and behaviour, if only because many ministers have at some time or another belonged to a College Christian Union. Its publishing imprint (IVP—InterVarsity Press) has been highly effective since the 1950s, producing a stream of impeccably orthodox books on almost everything from sex to sociology and ethics to ethnicity. Its Tyndale Bible Commentaries are on every evangelical minister's bookshelf; its excellent one-volume Bible commentary is the standard birthday present for every devout evangelical teenager. Probably the emergence of a genuine evangelical scholarship was the distinctive mark of evangelicalism in the fifties and sixties. It certainly took many liberal Christians by surprise. The mark of the seventies and eighties has almost certainly been the influence of the charismatic movement, both positively (in its effect on worship, preaching and teaching) and negatively (in the sharp reaction to it in the reformed ranks).

The seventies were also marked by a much sharper divide between Anglican Evangelicals and the rest, following the two national assemblies at which they committed themselves with fresh enthusiasm to the renewal of the Church of England by involvement rather than withdrawal. Other Evangelicals were unhappy about this. Those, like the Westminster Fellowship group, who had always doubted the theological reliability of the Anglicans, saw it as proof of their compromising tendencies. They were probably in their heart of hearts relieved to see the issue so clearly resolved: a rather sporadic war of words had spluttered along since the early sixties, when Dr Martyn Lloyd-Jones used an Evangelical Alliance rally to call on Anglican Evangelicals to leave the Church of England and align themselves with other Evangelicals. Two or three clergy responded to his call—one of whom later returned to the Church of England. Most Anglicans dismissed his invitation, but the Fellowship of Independent Evangelical Churches (FIEC) received a substantial boost as numbers of ministers from 'mainline' Free Churches joined their ranks. Indeed, the whole event seemed to clarify the renewal–withdrawal debate in a way Dr Lloyd-Jones could not have expected. It confirmed Anglican suspicions that they were not really accepted as *bona fide* Evangelicals by the 'reformed' party, and never would be. It served as a warning that they and their congregations were going to be under increasing pressure to abandon a 'doctrinally mixed' denomination and join a doctrinally 'pure' one—or at any rate an association of doctrinally pure Churches. This new realisation was an important factor in the attitude adopted at the Anglicans' National Evangelical Assembly at Keele in 1967, which signalled an important shift of emphasis. The quest for a doctrinally pure Church—the pot of gold at the foot of the evangelical rainbow—was to be abandoned. Instead, the great majority of Anglican Evangelicals (which means in practice probably half the Evangelicals in England) committed themselves to working within the Church of England, and also within the wider ecumenical movement.

Nothing could be more of an anathema to the Reformed party. Indeed, for most of them 'ecumenical' is virtually synonymous with 'heretical', and self-styled Evangelicals who have anything to do with the ecumenical movement put themselves beyond the pale. The monthly paper of the hard-line Reformed group, the *Evangelical Times*, has a quite remarkable nose for this kind of doctrinal deviation, sniffing out not only such obvious 'heretics' as Anglicans and Methodists, but also would-be members of its own constituency who are so careless as to fraternise with them. Hardly anybody since the eighteenth century is regarded as indisputably sound, and the letters column fairly rattles with exposés of this and that doctrinal deviation—nowadays often committed by the charismatics, who are in danger of pushing the ecumenists out of the coveted position of 'Reformed Enemy Number One'.

However, like most groups wedded to the chimera of total doctrinal purity, the Reformed party has itself suffered a major split. A tussle for control of the *Evangelical Times* put the paper firmly in the hands of the hard-liners, while those opposed to such rigid separationism launched a new paper, *Evangelicals Now*, with a more open attitude towards Christians in the mainstream Churches. This split has clarified the distinction between the separatist hard-liners within the British Evangelical Council and the Fellowship of Independent Evangelical Churches who are more open, especially to charismatics. Both, of course, stand for doctrinal purity, reject ecumenism and are generally critical of what they call 'doctrinally mixed' denominations.

This separatism is the predominant flavour of evangelicalism in Northern Ireland. Not all are as openly or stridently anti-Rome as Dr Ian Paisley, but the members of most of the thousands of mission halls and revivalist groups know very precisely who the enemies of the gospel are. A BBC journalist told me of an encounter with a very drunk Protestant in a Belfast street late at night. My colleague had to endure a long and eloquent speech, not about the need for twenty pence for a cup of tea but about the evils of the ecumenical movement (and try saying *that* when you are drunk!).

But this kind of hard-line Protestant evangelicalism is demonstrably a fading force in English Christianity. There are probably considerably fewer than 100,000 people in membership with the FIEC and BEC-linked churches. In contrast, the Baptist Union has about 200,000 members, the Black-led Churches (mostly evangelical) 66,000 members (though many more attend), the traditional Pentecostal Churches 78,000, the Salvation Army 60,000, the Christian Brethren 70,000 and the House Church movement perhaps 100,000. It is hard to estimate how many people are members of evangelical Anglican Churches, simply because there is strictly speaking no such thing, but the best estimate I can obtain is that about 400,000 people attend Anglican Churches where the ministry is evangelical. Add all of these together and you do indeed arrive at the Evangelical Alliance statistic of a million evangelical Christians in the United Kingdom.

They divide, as we have seen, into a number of sectors, and it takes something like a Billy Graham mission to bring the bulk of them together. The Anglicans are probably the largest group. Baptists (Union and 'free') are undoubtedly second, overlapping with the Reformed group. The charismatic movement involves many people in the mainline churches, of course, but shares much of its theology and experience with the Pentecostal Churches, most House Churches and many of the Black-led churches. The Christian Brethren have retained their distinctively lay approach to worship and ministry and continue to co-operate with other Evangelicals in many places. They are, however, mostly fairly wary of charismatic phenomena, and this has brought internal tensions.

As can be imagined, it is not easy for the great interdenominational movements and societies to embrace this new variety. TEAR Fund, founded in the early 1960s by the Evangelical Alliance, is one that manages to do so, largely because it restricts its activities to world-wide relief and development work. London Bible College, too, is widely respected, though the staff have to work hard to avoid fuelling controversy between the various groups on the campus. The same is true of the UCCF and Scripture Union: the price of broad support is eternal vigilance since there are plenty of people who would like to hijack such movements for their own ends.

I have several times mentioned Spring Harvest, and it is a phenomenon deserving of attention. In many ways it epitomises much modern evangelicalism. Sponsored by *Twenty-first Century Christian* magazine and British Youth for Christ, it currently fills two enormous holiday camps for three weeks in the spring of each year: Somerwest World at Minehead and Funcoast World at Skegness. Spring Harvest *is* fun, but it is also deadly serious, with seminars on moral, ethical and pastoral issues, Bible exposition and workshops on music, dance and drama. It draws many families and huge numbers of teens and twenties.

The theology of Spring Harvest is interdenominational evangelical, but with strong charismatic elements. Some of the leaders and speakers are Anglicans or Baptists. Others are prominent figures in the House Church or restoration movement. The result is a mix of styles and theologies, but the public face, especially at the big evening meetings, is of an excitable, somewhat triumphalist kind of evangelicalism, charismatic in style if not entirely in theology.

Many of its founders and organisers are supporters of the Argentinian-born evangelist Luis Palau, who has said of Spring Harvest that he has not seen 'anything more significant' in all his world travels. Palau has conducted several large-scale missions in Britain—twice in Wales, once in Scotland and (coinciding with Billy Graham's Mission England) once in London. He did not endear himself to some Anglican Evangelicals in London, and their support for his campaign was patchy, at best. He is not a man given to self-doubts, at any rate in public, and is not averse to scoring a few points off assorted and often unnamed theologians and intellectuals before getting down to the meat of his message.

When he sticks to the *kerygma* (the apostolic gospel), he is an effective evangelist. Like Billy Graham in earlier times, however, he does feel bound to comment in dogmatic terms about almost any issue pushed at him by the media, and this undermines his own credibility and that of his evangelistic message. This is partly a consequence of the lionisation in some circles of evangelists. In fact, as both Palau and Graham frequently assert, they are simply 'messenger boys'. In which case, much the wisest course, surely, is to stick to the message.

Spring Harvest has a certain flavour of Palau about it, both in its good and its weaker points. That it has stimulated and renewed many Christians is beyond any doubt. There are congregations up and down the country that have been enormously encouraged by the returning delegates of Spring Harvest. It has, in many cases, 'equipped the Church to serve the nation', as its current slogan claims. But it is a high-pressure, fizzy kind of religious experience, which has a sad tendency to go flat when exposed to the doubts, hesitations and difficulties of the real world, even the real church world.

Not every minister is overjoyed to find his Spring Harvest contingent insisting on a forty-minute sequence of praise songs (accompanied by computerised keyboard, guitar and percussion) before the morning service can get properly under way. If he gives in to them, his resident congregation feels assaulted. If he does not, he is in danger of being regarded as basically unspiritual.

Of course, this is a peril of all revival movements, and of crusade-style evangelism. Somehow it *must* translate back into the actual world of Commercial Street Baptist Church and Lower Tidworth Gospel Hall. The speakers and organisers of Spring Harvest are, many of them, fully aware of the difficulty. But fifty or sixty thousand hyped-up Evangelicals create a heady mixture, not easily bottled up and shipped back to the home churches. This is no reason for abandoning events like Spring Harvest, of course. But it is a factor in evaluating their lasting influence on the Church and (according to that slogan) the nation.

I shall be looking at the restoration movement in a separate chapter, but it has to be said here that the presence both of leaders and members of these House Churches at events like Spring Harvest is an encouraging sign that the movement (in parts, at least) wants to be seen as *within* rather than completely outside the mainstream of church life. Gerald Coates and Peter Fenwick, for instance, have an admirable record of inter-church co-operation and genuinely respect the views of those Evangelicals who do not feel bound to join the Restoration movement.

Nevertheless, this within–without divide is an ever-present source of tension. So too is the public exercise of the *charismata*, the 'gifts of the spirit'—tongues, prophecy and interpretation. Evangelical churches have split, and are still splitting, over these issues, and big public events like Spring Harvest bring them into the open. Evangelicals have always had a self-destructive tendency to divide. It is probably a perverse consequence of their insistence on the 'right and duty of the private interpretation of Scripture', as the old doctrinal basis of the Evangelical Alliance used to put it. Churches have divided; leaders have left or been excommunicated, over such issues as the details of the Second Coming, the interpretation of the Book of Daniel, the right of women to pray in public, the opening of a church bookstall on Sundays or the precise manner of prayer for healing (should one say, 'If it is the Lord's will' or not?).

Over the centuries since the Reformation there seems to be little doubt that this tendency to split over secondary issues has weakened the influence of evangelicalism more than any other single issue. Darwinism or Higher Criticism did not deal the movement such devastating blows as it has inflicted upon itself. And even today, those who argue most fervently for evangelical unity (the Reformed party) in practice insist that it must be upon their terms.

Thus evangelicalism in Britain is a powerful force, numerically strong and growing, but unable to exert the influence it ought to have either within the Church (in its broadest sense) or in the nation. Evangelicals did manage to unite to oppose, successfully, the Sunday Trading Bill. It is probably significant that they were united only in what they were all against.

Time will tell in which direction the movement will grow. Are the Anglican Evangelicals right to put their main effort into the life and work of their own Church rather than inter-denominational movements? Indeed, can evangelicalism, as a distinctive spirituality, survive and flourish in a 'mixed' denomination? Or is the Reformed party right: that however small the remnant, it is their faithfulness to the revealed truth that matters, not their power or influence in society? Or do the charismatics have the answer: church order and even doctrine itself are less important than being open to the Spirit?

I think a detached observer of the present scene might want to hedge his bets. I admire the way that Anglican Evangelicals have developed a kind of Reformed catholic theology, discovering afresh the doctrine of the Church and finding plenty of room in it for that distinctive understanding of justification and rebirth that has always gone hand in hand with spiritual renewal. I admire the determination of the Calvinists, the openness and freedom of the Charismatics and the simple, biblical faith of the 'old-line' Evangelicals. Perhaps in the end it is part of the providence of God that so important an element of Christianity should be contained in such strangely contrasting packages. 'But we have this treasure in jars of clay.'

CHAPTER NINE

THE CHARISMATICS

RATHER LIKE THE EVANGELICALS, Charismatics are involved in almost every area of Christian life. They are present in all the traditional Churches— in the Roman Catholic, Anglican and Baptist Churches, in the House Churches, in the various Pentecostal groupings, in the Black-led churches and in various community fellowships. One Church of England bishop, responsible for about 120 churches, told me a few years ago that there was not one of them that did not have a charismatic presence, even if it was limited to a single worshipper.

In this chapter, as in the previous one, I should like to try to assess the movement as a distinct if variegated grouping within Christendom. But this is harder to do, partly because the spectrum is broader (I do not know of any evangelical Roman Catholics, for instance) and partly because there are few, if any, umbrella organisations bringing together the great majority of Charismatics. In the early days of the movement in its modern form the Fountain Trust did manage to unite a very wide range of church traditions, from House Church to Roman Catholic, but it exists no more, and nothing has taken its place.

What we are left with is the charismatic experience. Even that is interpreted differently by different groups. But the particular gifts that are its hallmark are common ground: *glossolalia* (speaking in tongues) and its interpretation, prophecy and healing.

The experience, and the gifts, have been present off and on

in the Church throughout its history, so far as can be told. Certainly the Montanists, 1,600 years ago, and the Irvingites, a century ago, spoke in tongues and prophesied. The modern pentecostal movement began at the turn of this century with an outbreak of charismatic phenomena in an Anglican church in Sunderland and the eccentric but memorable ministry of an itinerant preacher called Smith Wigglesworth.[1] For a long while it flirted with the traditional Churches, but, largely because they rejected it, pentecostalism (as it was known) became denominational, and the original groups still exist, and are growing: the Assemblies of God and the Elim Church.

Their differences are of church order. The Assemblies are independent and congregational, Elim is connexional and (more or less) presbyterian. They have both had some outstanding ministers over the years, (men like Douglas Quy and George Canty) but it took the wider charismatic movement to bring the doctrine and experience into the public arena.

The transition began in the late 1950s in America, when several congregations in the traditional Churches—notably an episcopalian one in Houston—experienced what they tended to call 'baptism in the Holy Spirit' and began to explore the charismatic gifts. News of these events soon reached Britain, where there had already been a good deal of talk about revival. The two ideas coalesced. The answer to spiritual indifference was the fire of the Holy Spirit.

What was absolutely new about this movement, compared to all the previous revivalist movements since the Wesleys, was the impact that it made on the Church of England and the Roman Catholic Church. A curate at the well-known evangelical church of All Souls, Langham Place, in London's West End, was 'baptised in the Spirit' as he drove his car. He found himself praying in tongues. Michael Harper became a pivotal figure in the new movement and the leader of the Fountain Trust, the main melting-pot for the new Pentecostalists. Over the following years many distinguished ministers and church leaders joined the movement, though in truth there was nothing to join. Priests and nuns led charismatic prayer groups in many parishes. Speaking in tongues and

---

[1] His biography, *Baptised by Fire*, by Jack Hywel Davies (Hodder) is worth reading.

prophecy (uttering a message regarded as of direct divine origination) became quite common in many churches. Michael Green (then principal of St John's Theological College, Nottingham), David McInnes (then of Birmingham Cathedral), John Collins (then at St Mark's, Gillingham) and, most notably of all, David Watson (St Michael-le-Belfrey, York) gave substance and presence to the movement in the Church of England. Apart from an American, Jean Darnall, there were few women prominent in the leadership. Whether this was a decision of the Holy Spirit, or out of deference to male sensitivities, it is not possible to say.

However, by the early 1970s the charismatic renewal had clearly come to stay. Its magazine, *Renewal*, was widely read. Its leaders were well known in the Church. It had patrons in high places: Cardinal Suenens of Belgium was an open supporter and Pope Paul VI gave charismatic delegates an encouraging reception at a special Mass on Pentecost Sunday 1975. At the Lambeth Conference in 1978 scores of bishops from many countries were happy to align themselves with the renewal movement.

The separation of the House Churches from the mainline charismatics does not seem to have inhibited a steady growth in the movement. Although the Fountain Trust wound itself up and there are now fewer large-scale spectacular events on a national level, there continues to be impressive evidence of grass-roots advance. A large number of Anglican ordination candidates are charismatic—as many as half in some colleges. The movement has had remarkable penetration among priests and nuns in the Republic of Ireland, and the effect has begun to cross the Irish Sea. Charismatic songs are sung in churches of all kinds, even those that are suspicious of charismatic theology.

Interestingly, the movement has never been exclusively evangelical. It seems to have a particular appeal to some groups of catholics and has led to one or two astonishing 'conversions' among liberal clergy. It does not demand a fundamentalist view of the Bible, but those liberals who have shared the charismatic experience have invariably moved towards a more conservative view of the Bible. Conversely, some fundamentalists have found that it has freed them from literalism and given them a more dynamic view of revelation.

Many commentators feared that the charismatic movement would split the traditional Churches. It is true that individual congregations have experienced division, sometimes bitter and fierce. But that phase seems to be passing, and many Churches contrive to hold together charismatic and non-charismatic members without too many difficulties. Certainly there has been no wholesale disruption. For instance, most bishops with whom I have discussed the matter are appreciative of the enthusiasm, commitment and loyalty of charismatic clergy and congregations.

There is an interesting parallel with the evangelical revival in the eighteenth century. The initial movement spread rapidly and affected large numbers of people very profoundly. There was a considerable amount of opposition, but the movement's most effective enemies were within its own ranks: division among its leaders and a sectarian attitude among many of its followers. The result, over a period of a hundred years, was two-fold. A distinct and influential evangelical presence had been established in British Christianity, in a way it had never been before. But its presence was fragmented, spread over seven or eight distinct and even competitive groupings, with a substantial 'rump' left in the Church of England. Today, over two hundred years later, that is still so. Evangelicalism could have dominated the Christian scene in Britain. That it did not was more the fault of its friends than its enemies.

I believe much the same is true of the charismatic movement. The objections to it from outside are mainly theological (concerning 'baptism in the Holy Spirit' and the place of prophecy, especially, in the Church today). Arguments over such issues are fairly arcane: unlikely to discourage someone who on other grounds felt drawn to the movement. What do discourage people from joining, and lead others to leave it, are its internal weaknesses—features that often seem to have little to do with its real message. There is, for instance, a tendency to spiritual arrogance: leaders and speakers are publicly referred to as 'Spirit-filled'; words of prophecy are given in practice a status at least equal to Scripture; miracles are claimed (almost demanded) in a way that suggests the claimants have the power to manipulate the will of God. That, at least, is how it seems to outsiders.

Then there is sometimes a strange lack of judgement (again,

as it appears to the observer) about what is important and what is trivial. I have watched a dozen people spend an hour 'rebuking' a headache that could have been dismissed by a couple of aspirin in five minutes. I have listened to well-heeled middle-class residents of the stockbroker belt invoking divine aid in such matters as the purchase of a house with a fifth bedroom, place for a son at a public school or the acquisition of an au pair. One noted charismatic priest, Colin Urqhart, has actually recorded an incident when (as he believes) the Lord miraculously provided him with a glass of orange juice on a jet flight—he cannot *stand* grapefruit. At one time there was a positive obsession with leg-lengthening (it is said that most people have one leg slightly longer than the other). It was regarded as a sign of 'taking authority' to be able to command the shorter leg to extend to the length of the other one.

All of this trivialises the work of the Holy Spirit in the eyes of many people, including many within the charismatic movement. It does sometimes seem that some hitherto perfectly sane people lose all sense of proportion following a charismatic experience. Every minor human ill is demonic; every minor daily coincidence is a miracle. That is probably less serious than an obsessive concern for personal happiness, health and satisfaction, as though our own well-being is the supreme effect of salvation. A constant analysis of one's spiritual, mental or physical health is hardly the hallmark of apostolic Christianity.

It would, however, be totally unfair to give the impression that all, or most, Charismatics are arrogant, self-centred, unbalanced or obsessive. In my estimation most are devout, even intense Christians who have had a particularly vivid experience of the Holy Spirit, an experience which subsequently colours everything in their lives. For some, this experience has awoken a dormant social conscience. For others, it has released unexpected gifts of music, eloquence or art. Like all powerful forces, this kind of experience is more easily accepted than controlled, so it is not surprising that every now and then someone is knocked off his emotional balance by it. But to stigmatise the whole charismatic movement, as some have done, as crazy and self-indulgent on the basis of its lunatic fringe is simply wrong.

What is undeniable, I think, is the movement's inbuilt tend-ency to division, a tendency it shares with most revivalist movements, including the Wesleyan. It is not simply a matter of the division between the renewal movement (with its aim of renewing the historic Churches through charismatic blessing) and the restoration movement (which aims to create a new kind of church structure based on the restoration of the gifts of the Spirit), though that is deep and wide. The participants in a major conference of charismatic leaders at Herne Bay as long ago as 1965 'were not content to settle for charismatic prayer groups on the fringe of the church's life. They were calling for fully committed fellowships (churches) where the whole way of life was submitted to the Lordship of Jesus through the power of the Spirit.'[1] This aim to create a new kind of church structure was not and is not the vision of those who are looking for the Holy Spirit to renew the Roman Catholic, Anglican and Free Churches.

The question of church structure is probably the main cause of division, but not by any means the only one. As we have seen, not all the House Churches accept the restoration position. Some are very unhappy about aspects of discipling. Some are willing to co-operate with traditional Churches in evangelism and social protest; others are not prepared to compromise on this. Charismatic churches have split, as did the large Millmead Church at Guildford in 1984. Theological and spiritual reasons are given, but sometimes one suspects personalities are crucial. The movement tends to create heroes, but also tends to destroy them. 'Spirit-filled' pastors, elders and apostles are not expected to show normal human fallabili-ties. It is a problem that the papacy has wrestled with for over a thousand years.

Doctrinal divisions have centred on terminology (what should the initial experience of the gifts be called?) and prac-tice (should baptism be in the name of the Trinity or 'Jesus only'?). The place of women has caused division. So have different views on healing. I watched, horrified, as a charis-matic congregation tore itself into two almost literally over the death bed of its minister. Should they pray for his physical healing, or for his physical healing *if it were the will of God*?

---

[1] According to Peter Hocken, *Streams of Renewal* (Paternoster Press, Exeter, 1986).

'God matters to the people of Northern Ireland, Catholic and Protestant.' Its Church leaders also matter, among them Robin Eames, Church of Ireland Archbishop of Armagh. See Chapter 11.

Photo: Keith Ellis

With the rising interest in religious news the BBC's Religious Affairs Correspondent has a key role. Rosemary Hartill took over from Gerald Priestland in 1982. See Chapter 13.

Photo: Keith Ellis

The Church of England's General Synod in session: 'It has established itself as an important forum for debate.' See Chapter 14.

'Graham has raised the visibility of Christianity in Britain': Billy Graham preaching at Earls Court, 1967. See pages 54–57.

Two Christian 'household names': Singer Cliff Richard
(left) and evangelist Billy Graham.

Photo: Church of England Newspaper

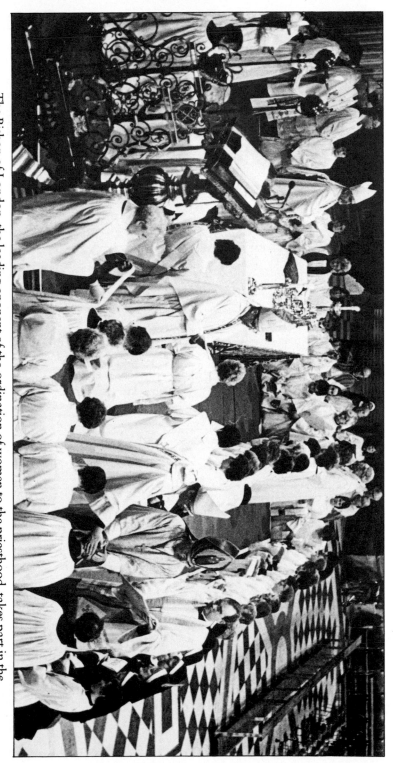

The Bishop of London, the leading oponent of the ordination of women to the priesthood, takes part in the ordination of seventy women deacons in St. Paul's Cathedral, 1987. 'The role of women is already a major cloud in the Church sky'. See Chapter 16.

Archbishop Derek Worlock, Bishop David Sheppard, and Moderator of the United Reformed Church Dr Newton — Pentecost Sunday 1987.

'People are turning to retreat houses because it is increasingly difficult to find the space or silence necessary ... to hear the voice of God.' Scargill Retreat Centre in Yorkshire. See Chapter 17.

Many redundant churches, like this one in Yiewsley, Middlesex, have been demolished ...

Photo: Keith Ellis

... but many new ones, like this shared church a few miles away at Uxbridge, have been built.

Photo: Keith Ellis

More than semantics are involved, of course. But it is the penalty of certainty that it has no room to manoeuvre.

Probably the greatest division among Charismatics in the 1980s has focused on the teaching of an American, John Wimber. His ideas of 'power evangelism', in which the miraculous is called upon to complement and confirm the evangelistic message, caused a great stir in charismatic circles. As sound a charismatic scholar as Michael Green (then Rector of St Aldate's, Oxford) publicly questioned them, in an article in the *Church Times*, though subsequently affirming his general unity with Wimber on doctrine. Many moderate charismatic leaders were genuinely worried by the apparently manipulative element in his teaching—manipulating not only potential converts, but even attempting to manipulate God. Wimber, of course, strenuously denies this. He is doing no more than the apostles did, 'confirming the Word with signs'. He is impatient with an apologetic, defeated, failure-ridden Church and extols its opposite—a confident, victorious, successful and dynamic Church.

The charismatic movement—like the evangelical movement—for all its spectacular growth, has not made the impact either on the Church or the nation that it might have done, but the renewal has come to stay, both inside and outside the traditional Churches. But it seems less likely now than it did twenty years ago that it might capture the heart and soul of Christendom. There are many, like myself, who respect the new life, vitality and freedom that renewal has brought to traditional Churches, and admire the zeal and commitment of the House Church movement, but hold back from whole-heartedly endorsing either because of what we have seen in practice. I find the theological objections unconvincing, but any movement of the Spirit must also be judged by its fruits: and some of the fruits of the charismatic movement set the teeth on edge. It is not a matter of embarrassment at the expression of emotion, nor even hesitation about supernatural phenomena. Nor is it, in my case, opposition to the movement *per se*. I am unreservedly glad that it exists and is so widely present in the Church. It has taught me a great deal and opened me to new spiritual possibilities. But it is, for me, only a part of the truth, not the whole. It desperately needs the discipline of Scripture and Church to make it a positive, effective and balanced power for good. For that reason, I believe it is more likely eventually to make a lasting impact in the historic Churches—perhaps especially the Roman Catholic Church—than elsewhere: again, rather like the Wesleyan revival.

The charismatic movement has already had a profound effect on worship in almost all the Churches, as we have seen. Its music is now part of the heritage of Christian worship. It has taught leaders and congregations about body-language, about feeling as well as saying, about enthusiasm as well as order. Its most profound influence, however, may well in the end be on attitudes to healing. We live in a health-conscious age—to the point of obsession at times. My observation is that the teaching and practice about healing draw more people to charismatic fellowships than any other single thing.

It is not simply a matter of healing diseases and handicaps. More commonly what is on offer is deliverance: deliverance in theory from possession by evil, often personified as demons. In practice it is deliverance from such things as persistent migraine, odd pains of unknown origin, depression, anxiety and guilt. There is no doubt that many people have received more effective help from spiritual healing than they have from psychiatry. I have myself met people who have been delivered from depression and anxiety: one person from a mental illness that had led to her being committed to Rampton Special Hospital. In her case, it was the ministry of the London Healing Mission that brought her to a psychological normality no one could have predicted or expected, and her cure has now lasted several years. Success is not guaranteed, of course, and some of the success that is claimed seems to owe more to optimism than cold fact. But charismatic groups do tend to attract people with just these afflictions, and their ministry to them is often effective.

Medical experts are now less sceptical about this. Indeed, they are not unwilling to call in the aid of Christian healers from time to time, even in the area of possession. The Church as a whole, too, is less suspicious. After all, Jesus was a healer and commanded his followers to continue this part of his ministry (Lk 9:1). Thus churches that have no particular charismatic beliefs are often to be found offering specific prayer for those who are ill, including laying-on of hands. And they, too, have moments when astonishing things happen.

Generally speaking, the *style* of charismatic healing is distinctive. It includes such practices as 'rebuking' the affliction, 'binding' the malign power of a cancer, perhaps, or a migraine, and 'resting in the Spirit'. This last is a phenomenon that has no New Testament model but is endemic in charismatic circles. As a person is being prayed over, they fall to the ground, apparently in some kind of faint or trance. At one time I felt sure they were pushed—the healer often puts his hands on the subject's head. I also suspected that it was a case of collusion: the healer wanted them to fall (to prove something was happening) and they wanted to fall (to demonstrate that healing or deliverance was taking place). And I thought that an unhealthy hysteria was at the root of it all.

However, having had the opportunity to watch charismatic healing at work in the London Healing Mission, over a fairly protracted period, and involving perhaps a score of cases, I have changed my mind, on two of those issues at least. I know for certain that many of those who fall—'resting in the Spirit'—are *not* pushed. And I am satisfied that hysteria is not involved, at any rate in the normal sense of the word. Those who fall often go off into a deep and profoundly wholesome sleep, from which they come round (perhaps half an hour later) refreshed, relaxed and 'feeling better'. I have talked to many people after they have awoken, and not one had found the experience frightening, distressing or disturbing. Quite the contrary: it had often been exactly what they felt they needed. I think the charge of collusion is unproven, though probably on both sides there is an expectation, based on past experience, that it will happen. It is notable that most people who are 'resting in the Spirit' have either seen other people fall in this way, or have done so themselves.

When I asked the missioner, Andy Arbuthnot, for a scriptural authority for this phenomenon, he admitted that he did not have one. He simply observed that it usually happened in a healing ministry of this kind. It seems relatively harmless, at worst, and positively restorative, at best, so it is hard to disagree with him that there seems no serious reason for discouraging it.

What might profitably be discouraged is the high-profile, mass-audience healing rallies of some itinerant (and usually transatlantic) evangelists. In a place like the London Healing Mission, or in a local church or fellowship, healing is associated with long-term pastoral care. It takes place after counselling, preparation and prayer, and it is followed up carefully over a long period of time. That is a far remove from a healing rally in the Central Hall, Westminster, where people are urged to hobble up on to the stage, meet the evangelist briefly as he prays over them, and are then invited to throw away their crutches, supports, hearing aids and so on. The atmosphere is highly charged with emotion. To hold back or express doubts would be regarded as evidence of unbelief and spiritual obstinacy. There is no counselling and no follow-up, little human contact and no pastoral care. Second only to the appeal for the sick to receive healing is the appeal for everyone to open their purses, and sometimes the priority is reversed.

Even in this setting I would not dare to say that God never heals anyone. Indeed, I believe that he is always greater than our attempts to manipulate him; greater even than his sacraments. So it is not really surprising that occasionally people seem to receive great help and even healing from such rallies. But these do the pentecostal movement as a whole no credit at all, as many of its leaders recognise, and often are closer to show-biz than the things of the Spirit.

I would not want to end this chapter, however, on a negative note. As one wit pointed out, you do not counterfeit £12 notes. Only the real thing is worth imitating. I believe the charismatic renewal has at its heart a very real thing, perhaps the most real thing of all: the Holy Spirit—present, active and effective in the midst of God's people.

CHAPTER TEN

THE RESTORATION MOVEMENT

CHURCH HISTORY, ANCIENT AND MODERN, is
full of men and movements that were going to
restore the kingdom of God. Faced with a worldly,
compromising Church, evangelistic failure, national
corruption and widespread disillusion with established
religion (and those symptoms have been present in every
century of the Church's history somewhere), someone always
raises the clarion call, 'Let's get back to the apostolic ideal
... the New Testament ... the purity of the early Church.
Let's abandon these corrupt institutions, man-made and cler-
ically dominated. Let's abolish priestcraft, prelacy and pomp.
Let's cut loose from the chains of religion and restore the real
thing!'

And people always respond. It is a delightful prospect—to
follow an exciting, prophetic leader (or two) on a path that
leads to the sunlit uplands of spiritual success. In the early
Church they became Montanists. In the late Middle Ages,
Hussites. In Italy there were the Waldensians; in Britain the
Brownites and the Quakers. In the nineteenth century the
early Plymouth Brethren sounded the same notes and drew
the same response. So did the Irvingites, the charismatic ritualists who caused a great stir in middle-class Victorian drawing
rooms. Today it is what some loosely refer to as the House
Church movement, or as I shall prefer to call it,
restorationism.

By House Churches most people mean any group of Christians operating outside the traditional Churches, whether they

actually meet in houses or not. Restorationism is a distinct theological position, as we shall see, shared by most but not all of those who belong to House Churches. However, some, like Roger Forster of the Ichthus Fellowship, do not fit easily into either category, while sharing some aspects of both.

There is much to say that is good about all the movements I have mentioned, and about many, many others which with simple faith set out to pioneer a new path: one that leads back to the apostles and Jesus, and forward to a new age, the kingdom age he foretold, in which a restored Church, the faithful remnant, would joyfully welcome its returning Lord. But it has to be said that taken as a whole they represent a catalogue of lost causes, missed opportunities, disappointment and disillusion. All have left their mark on the catholic Church. All have contributed something to the sum total of mankind's spiritual quest. But they have not brought in the millenium. Indeed, most of them barely survived a hundred years except as a spent force.

Each movement, virtually without exception, has begun with a charismatic leader. Often he professed great loyalty to the Church; generally he rejected ideas of disruption and schism. Yet what has almost inevitably followed has been either schism or excommunication: his followers left, or they were thrown out. And again, almost without exception, as the movement became schismatic or detached, it slowly lost its original vision and became sectarian. Some, like the Irvingites, have simply disappeared into the annals of church history. Many, like the Brethren, continue as one of the very denominations they were once taught to reject. A few, like the Hussites and the Brownites, have been the catalysts by which major new forms of Christianity have come into being. In other words, it is a risky business being any kind of a reformer; it is a perilous one being the leader of a group which sets out to restore such elusive things as the faith and order of the apostolic Church.

Still, there has been no shortage of those prepared to have a try. They are not, as a group of people, noted for self-doubt, timidity or (let's be honest) humility. It does, after all, require something approaching arrogance to announce that everybody has got it wrong for 1,900 years, but that you have got it right. Yet it is that very arrogance, that sublime self-confidence, that gives the word 'faith' a new dimension, and a more exciting one than is offered week by week in ordinary Churches. It offers ordinary men and women the chance to be pioneers, to do something different and exciting, to share in a new vision of truth. Put less politely, it gives people a chance to have that lovely, warm feeling that they are absolutely right, and everybody else (including a lot of people they had hitherto been taught to look up to) absolutely wrong. You can see that feeling shining out of the eyes of the Jehovah's Witness or Mormon on your doorstep, but you can also see it in the eyes that gaze with rapture at the latter-day apostles who are leading them into battle to rebuild the kingdom of God.

I suppose that sounds a fairly cynical introduction to a chapter on the restoration movement. Indeed, in one way I *am* sceptical both about the nature of its appeal and the likelihood that it will replace the holy, catholic Church as the body of Christ on earth. But I am neither sceptical nor cynical about the genuine faith of many of its leaders and members (among them some of my own friends and relations) and I am conscious how much I personally owe to what might reasonably be called restoration movements of the past, including the Protestant Reformation, the Wesleyan revival and even the Brethren movement. The restorationists may not have *all* the truth, but they often represent a missing part of the truth, and it is often a part that the Church of the time has ignored and needs to accept.

The modern restoration movement had its beginnings in a strange fusion of Brethren and pentecostal ideas. Almost all of the men who shaped its early thinking had a Brethren background—Arthur Wallis, David Lillie, Denis Clarke and Campbell McAlpine, among others. This gave them a rooted dislike of denominationalism and clericalism (the idea of a paid, ordained, one-man ministry). But they had also all come under the influence of the new pentecostalism—the charismatic movement began to make its presence felt in Britain in the early 1960s—though some of these men also had had contacts with the older Pentecostal Churches. This gave to their theology a strongly revivalist flavour. They spoke of a world-wide 'latter rain' of blessing that would herald the return of Christ. As part of this revival, the old denominations

would wither away, and a new, universal, Spirit-filled Church
come into being.

A number of conferences in the 1960s brought together
various leading figures in the charismatic movement who were
dissatisfied with its theology of the Church. Basically, they
were not happy to see renewal simply as a lifeline for the
historic Churches. For them, the call was to create something
new. As Wallis saw it, the time had come for 'a larger coming
together to share the great vision that the Spirit of God is
unfolding . . . the Holy Spirit is wanting to work in apostolic
power through a fully functioning body, fed and led and
governed by spiritual elders.' So, at any rate, claimed a circular
calling a conference of his associates in New Zealand in 1964.

For many years, however, men like Wallis and McAlpine
remained in close contact with the charismatic movement in
its broadest manifestations; they were connected with the
Fountain Trust, for instance, which was non-denominational
but highly influential in Anglican and Roman Catholic circles.
But, according to Andrew Walker, author of the only serious
history yet written of the House Church movement, Wallis
was 'never at ease with those Anglican and Catholic Charismatics who seemed quite happy with infant baptism.' He
believed the renewal movement lacked 'discipline and
authority'.[1]

Slowly, and at first hidden by the surging waves of the
general charismatic movement, leading figures in it who had
themselves come from a separatist background—mostly
Brethren or Pentecostal—began to discuss openly the need
for a new church framework. One by one, in various parts
of the country (Chard in Somerset, Cobham in Surrey, and
around Bradford), House Churches were appearing. Most of
the members, like their leaders, were disaffected adherents of
non-aligned evangelical Churches. Remarkably few—I think
only Maurice Smith and Terry Virgo, among the leaders—
had ever belonged to the Church of England or the mainstream Free Churches. But as they came together in a series
of conferences, a theology of the 'restored kingdom' emerged.
They came to believe that they were the heralds, indeed,
literally the apostles, of a new kind of Church.

---

[1] *Restoring the Kingdom* (Hodder, 1985), p. 42.

By the early 1970s a London Brotherhood had been formed of leaders such as Gerald Coates, Terry Virgo, George Tarleton and Maurice Smith. A similar grouping was taking place in Yorkshire, around a former Assemblies of God pastor, Bryn Jones, and his brother Keri. Links with similar groups in the United States were forged, and the distinctive elements of restoration theology began to emerge.

Its basic principle was to liberate its members from the constraints of a dead religion: from traditional church order, liturgy, clericalism and formality. It wanted to create a truly charismatic fellowship. It sought a pattern of leadership— discipling, as it became known—that would guard the new movement from error and disunity. The rules and order of the Church would be based on two complementary revelations, the Scriptures (the word, or *logos*) and the word of prophecy (*rhema*). And the aim of it all was no less than to restore a 'glorious Church' that would itself signal the 'restoration of all things' with the return of Christ.

Now those are heady objectives in principle and a massive agenda in practice. The new apostles (at first seven, known to their followers as the 'magnificent seven', and later augmented to the 'fabulous fourteen') shared a sense of mutual destiny, expressed in a joint covenant. As their leadership was recognised, so more and more Churches put themselves under their authority. And that was a considerable step, for members were expected to abjure 'wilful independence' and submit to discipling in many areas of their lives. This authority is exercised by elders, who themselves are discipled by apostles. The apostles, in theory at least, disciple each other. It makes for a network of authority which, however lovingly exercised, contrasts with that primary aim of liberating the members. In practice, they do not seem very liberated, especially those who are in the more authoritarian groups (largely in the North of England): if the purchase of a new car or the taking out of an insurance policy are matters requiring church approval, liberation still seems a long way off. They are also no longer as united as they once were. In the 1970s several rifts developed, with at least two major groupings, with different views on discipline and order, and several minor ones, often divided by personalities.

But the movement has unquestionably grown. Its public

face—through the Capel Bible Week, the Dales Bible Week (now called 'Restoration'), among many other similar gatherings, and its books, tapes and videos—gives an impression of buoyant growth. Numbers at the holiday conferences are large, up to 8,000 or so at each—and enthusiastic. Yet in truth it is still a small movement, not much larger than the Brethren movement out of which it grew: at most 100,000 members or so. It gains members often by transfer: people leave their previous church—perhaps moving to a new home—and link up with the Restorationists. Some transfer on grounds of principle or doctrine. And nowadays quite a few are added by conversion, people whose first and only experience of the Christian Church is a restored fellowship.

It also loses members: not a large number, but often they are able people, even leaders. Some who were destined for ministry have been encouraged to study theology. Almost inevitably that has raised problems. It is hard to know much Church history and still regard these gathered 'remnant' fellowships as an adequate expression of the body of Christ. Others are put off by the movement's sectarian tendencies, reminiscent of the Brethren: a residual legalism about things like women wearing hats; an unrestrained chauvinism about leadership, which is almost exclusively male, and in some sections a puritanical morality.

So what is the appeal of the restoration movement? Clearly it meets a need. Nothing could grow so quickly over so brief a period without having an attractiveness of its own. Undoubtedly part of its appeal is the same as that of the charismatic movement in general: a freedom in worship, a warmth in association, moments of high emotion and plenty of colour and sound. Many of us have been deeply insulated by our upbringing and conditioning from such experiences. We sit or stand stiffly, wrap ourselves in our folded arms, keep our heads and hands down and are afraid to express our pent-up feelings in words or body language. There is no doubt that the charismatic experience has liberated many people. An interior release has set them free to sing their heads off, hold their hands high, weep (if they feel like it), shout aloud, hug and kiss each other and, on occasions, even dance in the aisles.

Restorationists are charismatic in practice, though some groups are actually fairly restrained in demonstrating it. Services are often extremely long. They feature the typical songs of the movement: simple, repetitive and scriptural in content, gentle 'pop' in musical style (often with heavy piano chords holding back the rhythm, creating a sense of pent-up emotion). The hallmark of the whole thing, though, is well summed up in a press release for 'Restoration 87' (one of twenty successors to the Dales Bible Week) under the caption 'Days of Destiny': 'The event, which is organised by a team of men led by Welsh-born Bryn Jones, is expected to include dynamic praise and worship, exciting teaching from the Bible and dramatic answers to prayer for healing.' That pretty well sums up the appeal of house church worship: dynamic ... exciting ... dramatic. Add in the hint of the miraculous ('answers to prayer for healing') and it is a heady mix, far removed either from the usual Free Church 'hymn sand-wich' or the liturgical worship of Roman Catholics and Anglicans.

The other chief appeal, I suspect, is the whole notion of discipling. Members are linked into a web of relationships within which each one is 'covered' by someone else, and once 'qualified', provide cover themselves for another member. To some people this sounds positively Orwellian. Try telling a typical Anglican congregation that the details of their daily lives—jobs, friendships, recreations, marriages—were to be subject to supervision by a designated church member! Yet for those who are drawn into this kind of fellowship it clearly provides a discipline, stability and reassurance in coping with life. Perhaps typically, members of House Churches are not self-confident, assured people. Perhaps they do need to be nurtured or shepherded. Whatever the explanation, discipling is a distinctive element in the Restoration Churches: probably *the* distinctive element. And it is this one that has evoked the most criticism, even from those who are basically sympathetic. Maurice Smith, for instance, sees it as 'legalism': 'striving for perfection, under delegated authority, leads to a sense of inadequacy and perhaps despair'. George Tarleton, who left the movement after many years as a leader, believes that 'the greatest damage was done by the submission trip which the leaders went on . . . Submission to men was imposed on the church . . . individuality was being strangled to death.'[1]

Interestingly, the leaders of the House Church movement as a whole are almost all able men, but not intellectuals. The best theological thinker among them, in my opinion, is Roger Forster, founder of the Ichthus Fellowship (which is not really in the restoration camp). It bands together twenty-two 'congregations', some of which retain links with the traditional denominations—one belongs to the London Baptist Association, for instance. The general ethos, however, is very definitely that of both renewal and restoration. Most of the other leaders are sharp, articulate, persuasive and very confident, but with little sense of history. They 'know their Bible', in the sense of knowing what is in it, but they interpret it in a doctrinaire way. When they get hold of an idea it can be very hard to persuade them to adapt or relate it to any other idea, especially, I suspect, if it appears to undermine their argument. They are leaders, in the sense that people follow them, but they are not, I think, spiritual giants. Those who follow them are good, honest Christian people, many of them successful in business; but few, in my experience, have the intellectual equipment to challenge the selective exegesis and tendentious theology which is often on offer.

If precedent is anything to go by (and it usually is, in church history), then the restoration movement will cause the established Churches a few headaches for the next couple of decades but lose its impetus as it splits into different factions, as the mainstream Churches steal its creative ideas (as they have already adopted much of its music), and as some of its leaders find new ideas and avenues to pursue. It is always hard for innovators to settle down to the task of consolidation. Inevitably there will be setbacks and disappointments which some of them may be temperamentally ill-equipped to combat.

However, some of the House Churches do have the qualities required for long-term survival. Mostly they are those that are not built around one charismatic personality and have an open, flexible approach: the Sheffield Community is one. It organised a National Women's Day in 1987 to enable

---

[1] Quoted by Andrew Walker, *Restoring the Kingdom* (Hodder, 1985), p. 275–6.

women to be 'more effective in today's Church'. Others are painstakingly reappraising their approach. It is certainly possible that the House Churches will eventually become an official part of British Christendom, like the early Pentecostal Churches and the Brethren. But that is hardly the stuff millenial dreams are made of.

For the present, they represent the only genuinely new, radical form of Christianity on offer in Britain. Their desire to rebuild the kingdom and bring back the King has involved them in a number of exercises aimed at arousing the national conscience and challenging secular attitudes and values. The Festival of Light in 1971 was seen by many of them as the first public attempt to raise a banner against the forces of darkness that opposed the kingdom. A march on the City of London in 1987 was a strange sequel to it: Christians paraded with banners and drums to 'claim the City for Christ' and oppose the rampant evils of greed and injustice for which (they felt) the City was noted.

But the leaders know that such events are merely icing on the cake. What counts is the depth of commitment of the members, their sense of purpose and destiny, and, perhaps most of all, the quality of the leadership. By normal human criteria the House Churches are here to stay, at least for the foreseeable future. They would say, of course, that other criteria apply to them and that in any case the foreseeable future may not be very long: and who is to say that they are wrong?

CHAPTER ELEVEN

THE CELTIC LANDS

CHRISTIANITY WAS REBORN IN THESE ISLANDS through the Celtic Church 1,300 years ago. Today it is still stronger in the three Celtic lands than in the Anglo-Saxon one: churchgoing in England is probably about 10 per cent, nearly twice as high in Wales, more than twice as high in Scotland, and at least three times higher in Northern Ireland. But it is probably simplistic to deduce from that that England is once again due to be re-evangelised from the west and north. On the whole, most of the English are pretty wary of the various brands of Christianity on offer in the Celtic countries, categorising the Welsh as hymn-singing romantics, the Scots as dour conservatives and the Northern Irish as bickering bigots. Let me hasten to say that those are caricatures, and I speak as someone who has owed a great deal to that part of my religious upbringing which took place in Wales. However, as with all caricatures, there is a hint of truth in all three.

WALES

Christianity in Wales is probably just recovering from the effects of the Welsh revival of eighty years ago. While this led to an enormous upsurge of religious enthusiasm, much of it seems to have been somewhat hysterical in character and (unlike other religious revivals of history) to have had little long-term impact on the life of the nation. It gave Wales hundreds more enormous chapels to add to the ones it already had, great monsters of brick and slate which dominate the valleys and litter the countryside. For a while some of them were full, but soon after World War I they were emptying fast, and today many are redundant. Worse than that, the revival has left a certain cynicism about chapel religion among Welsh people. They like the hymns, still turn up for a *Cymanfa Ganu* and know the words well enough to bawl them into the sky at the National Stadium. But many of them identify with the cynical picture of chapel minister and deacons portrayed in works like *Under Milk Wood*. Yet this cynicism is a cover, an excuse. The Welsh are a naturally 'religious' people. They need a *reason* for not belonging to a church, and the real or imagined hypocrisy of past or present believers is the most commonly expressed excuse.

Today, however, religion of a fairly serious kind is making a comeback in Wales. The Evangelical Movement of Wales, a body which holds the memory and principles of Dr Martyn Lloyd-Jones in profound reverence, is strong and growing, especially among students and graduates. It is definitely serious: it will not trifle with compromise, especially with the ecumenical movement or the Church of Rome. It has able preachers in its ranks, a clear objective and an unambiguous basis of faith. It would *not* subscribe to the view that the Welsh revival was a flash in the pan, though some of its adherents are a bit doubtful about the way the revival later developed. It has a vigorous publishing programme and organises conventions, study weekends and ministers' conferences. Strangely, though, it has been much more successful among the English-speaking than the Welsh-speaking people.

The general Free Church scene in Wales is complicated both by the issue of language and by a serious rift over theology. The language issue is easier to describe. Welsh, an ancient, beautiful and highly inflective language, has long retained its hold on Christian worship in Wales. In fact the Bible and Prayer Book in Welsh kept the language alive during the centuries when the English were trying to stamp it out. Today it is Welsh hymns, more than anything else, that keep the nation's language on the lips of its largely non-Welsh-speaking citizens. Many people who could not order a newspaper in Welsh can sing '*Calon Lân*' (a hymn about having a pure heart) or '*Dechrau Canu*' (about heavenly worship), and virtually everyone in Wales can manage the Lord's Prayer ('*Ein Tad . . .*'). So there is an emotional attachment which links the Welsh-speaking chapels with the Welsh-speaking people. Indeed, the Welsh Language Movement (Cymdeithas y Iaith Cymraeg) draws much of its support from ministers of religion and their congregations.

But it is an observable fact that these congregations include relatively few young people. Most of the growing churches are English speaking, and evangelical in theology. The Welsh churches are, for the most part, struggling to survive, even in the traditional strongholds of the language in the far west and north of Wales. There is a serious shortage of young ministers and a desperate need for a strategy that looks beyond mere survival. If the Welsh chapels are to be cast in the role of cultural museums or centres of political protest, then it is hard to see any real future for them as living churches. On the other hand, where congregations have begun to look out at the needs of those around them, especially in rural areas, it can be seen that renewal is possible. Playgroups, language schools, job creation schemes, youth clubs and old people's day centres are desperately needed and provide genuine points of contact with a largely unchurched population: and that is as true in the Welsh-speaking and mostly rural areas as anywhere else.

The theological issue is harder to analyse. The Evangelical Movement of Wales has undoubtedly begun to shift the theological climate. Much chapel theology has been of a very liberal variety, tinged with socialism and political protest. Indeed, some chapels, particularly in the congregationalist tradition, have become virtually unitarian. This is true in both English and Welsh congregations, though more widespread probably in the latter. The Presbyterian Church of Wales, once the stronghold of Reformed theology, has moved in the same direction and—coincidentally or consequently— has lost members at a rather higher rate than most other denominations.

Wales has been more positive, however, in ecumenical progress, all its major Churches being committed to a covenant scheme for eventual unity. However, this very scheme is the main or most ostensible reason for the unwillingness of the evangelical groups to associate with the main-line Churches. The very word 'ecumenical' is used as a weapon: those who support ecumenism are, by definition, 'unsound'. This has polarised churches in Wales, with little genuine dialogue between liberals and Evangelicals of the kind that occurs in the major denominations in England.

Wales: Churches

	Members	Ministers	Churches
Church in Wales	115,896	698	1,450
Roman Catholic	146,673	200	324
Methodist	22,561	193	415
Presbyterian	84,750	268	1,212
Baptist	45,611	245	785
Welsh Independents	65,200	210	746

The Roman Catholic Church is growing in Wales, though mostly by immigration rather than conversion. However, the growth is considerable, and has been taken to justify the creation of a second Welsh diocese. It is still a relatively small church—still smaller, proportionately, than its sister churches in Scotland and Northern Ireland. But it has made a belated attempt to come to terms with Welsh culture and interests, with the Mass celebrated in Welsh, Welsh hymns and an enthusiastic reinstatement of a large number of hitherto obscure Welsh saints.

The Church in Wales, which has suffered for two centuries from its connection with the hated English Establishment, is making a more surprising advance. It was the first Anglican Church in the United Kingdom to ordain women deacons; it is more involved ecumenically than the others; and it has arrested its decline sooner than the rest, church attendance having increased significantly in the last ten years. It has problems recruiting and training enough Welsh-speaking clergymen, but there is a notable growth of confidence among its members and some astonishingly fast-growing congregations. I think of a seaside village in West Wales with a population of 900, where the parish church fairly often has a congregation of over 200—well over 20 per cent. There are village churches with lively young congregations. There are several parishes where charismatic renewal has brought dramatic results. And the diocese of St David's—an almost entirely rural one—embarked on a year of mission in the summer of 1987 that was launched with a rally of 9,000 people: quite an achievement when the population of the cathedral 'city' is less than 2,000.

In contrast, the great Free Churches of Wales are still beset with problems of numerical decline. There are many able—indeed, brilliant—ministers. The preaching is still impressively eloquent. The singing is also good, though not quite as good as popular mythology would have us believe. And there are perhaps a score of large and growing congregations. But there has been a general drift away from the chapels—Congregationalists, Baptist, Methodist and Presbyterian. This is especially marked among young people and men. Many a massive rural chapel is kept going by a small band of dedicated older women, the loyal guardians of a great tradition. But it is a fearful struggle, and every time it fails another ugly symbol of defeat is created: a carpet warehouse, car showroom or craft centre based in what was once the house of God.

Yet the Welsh nonconformist tradition continues to dominate the religious landscape. Wales is an independently minded country, and the local autonomy, doctrinal freedom and disputatious style of the chapel suits its people. They may not go as often as they once did, and they may criticise the ministers and officers bitterly, but underneath it all there is a cultural bond that has not been dissolved.

SCOTLAND

In Scotland churchgoing is still more widespread than in Wales. There is, of course, a much larger Roman Catholic community, and Mass attendance is relatively high. But the Church of Scotland also still musters substantial congregations, especially outside the great urban areas, and in the more remote rural districts church attendance often involves more than half the population.

Since the Reformation, Christianity has presented itself in Scotland in three main forms: Roman Catholic, Presbyterian and Episcopalian. The Presbyterian element is, of course, by far the largest. The Church of Scotland, known everywhere simply as 'the Kirk', emerged in 1560 as a distinctive national Church in the Reformed tradition and rapidly developed the system of presbyterian government, which it still follows today. A system of courts or councils (of which the annual General Assembly is the chief and the Kirk session the local) replaced the pre-Reformation hierarchy of archbishop, bishops, and priests. The form of government takes its name from the 'presbytery', a court which covers a number of parishes and consists of all the qualified ministers together with an equal number of 'elders'—the senior lay officers of the Kirk. The chairman of the national General Assembly, held in Edinburgh every May, is known as the Moderator, and he holds office for one year only.

Scotland: Churches

	Members	Ministers	Churches
Presbyterian	901,914	1,513	2,142
Roman Catholic	285,554	1,111	478
Episcopalian	37,000	240	315
Baptist	17,666	175	190
Methodist	7,008	34	73

The Kirk has almost a million members in just over 2,000 congregations. The three smaller churches that broke away from the Church of Scotland between 1843 and 1900 are the Free Church, with about 180 congregations; the United Free Church (about 80); and the Free Presbyterian Church (about 40). There is also a very small but ancient Reformed Presbyterian Church with a few hundred members. Scotland has a small but active Baptist presence, with about 20,000 members and adherents.

The Episcopal Church in Scotland (Anglican) also dates back to the Reformation. The 'Piskies', as they are known, have been regarded by most Scots over the centuries as an English eccentricity, but in the last decade or so the Church has begun to attract attention and members, notably through some live and growing congregations in the big cities. It has over 300 congregations and about 70,000 members and adherents. Its main asset in recent years, however, has been the quality of its leadership, notably two scholar-bishops, Richard Holloway and Michael Hare-Duke.

Like Britain's other mainstream Churches, the Kirk is experiencing a resurgence of conservative evangelicalism. A large number of tutors and students in theology faculties are Evangelicals, and they have recently opened a centre, Rutherford House, for theological research and support, rather like Latimer House, Oxford, in England. The liberals, once so dominant, feel themselves under considerable threat. Indeed, one distinguished minister remarked ruefully that if he were president of the Bishop of Durham Fan Club he would be hard pressed to name a dozen possible members among the Kirk's 1,500 ministers.

The charismatic movement, on the other hand, has made relatively little progress. Dour evangelical Scots are anxious to assert the reality of miracles two thousand years ago, but are less convinced about the same things happening today. And in any case, even if they did, why should people get hysterical about it? The Scottish temperament and charismatic style do not seem to go well together.

Ecumenically things are as static as they seem to be elsewhere in the United Kingdom. Despite optimistic conferences and fine words from church leaders, all most people expect to see are some revised 'ecumenical instruments'—an ugly phrase that is really a fancy way of describing councils of Churches. Perhaps the Roman Catholic Church will take a more positive role in the future, but it is highly unlikely that it could include the elements asked for by the 'Not Strangers but Pilgrims' questionnaires—notably, intercommunion. Even the baptism of the infant child of a kirk minister and his wife by their friendly local Roman Catholic priest was frowned on by the hierarchy: it 'confused the laity'.

NORTHERN IRELAND

Still, in Scotland the two great Churches—and that is overwhelmingly the situation—are at least on generally friendly terms. In Northern Ireland the divide is more glacial. Individual priests and ministers and groups of lay people may get on well together, meeting for prayer, Bible study and meditation, but in general the two communities, Protestant and Roman Catholic, have little to do with each other.

The predominant flavour of Protestantism in Ulster is also presbyterian, but that covers a wide spectrum, from liberal ecumenists to Paisleyite fundamentalists. Some of the strongest invective of the latter group is reserved for the leading figures of the former: much stronger, by and large, than they use about Roman Catholics. Undoubtedly most of the largest Churches, in terms of membership, are the more conservative ones. Northern Ireland Protestants have always been in the forefront of foreign missions and they still provide a large number of missionaries. There is still a growing pentecostal movement and also a strong pietist one, with conventions on holiness and the spiritual life. So it would be wrong to think of all Ulster Protestantism, even in its most evangelical manifestation, as uniformly strident and bigoted.

Northern Ireland: Churches

	Members	Ministers	Churches
Roman Catholic	353,014	549	420
Presbyterian	274,737	532	595
Church of Ireland	157,000	364	440
Methodist	20,792	244	126
Baptist	8,000	70	85

There is, after all, a strong evangelical element in the mainline Churches, too. The Church of Ireland, one of the most uniformly low church provinces of the Anglican Communion, has a number of evangelical parishes, as well as a few rather self-conscious high church ones. Its clergy are for the most part able, broad-minded men, and several of its bishops are outstanding, but it is a couple of decades behind its sister Church in England where liturgical renewal and mission are concerned. The Presbyterian Church of Ireland—which, like the Anglican one, straddles the border—also has an able and well-educated ministry, with well-kept plant, flourishing church clubs and organisations and strong lay leadership. It is under pressure all the while from its right wing, however, and has not been able entirely to fulfil earlier hopes that its

leaders would be able to create an alternative and more open
Protestant option in the province. Many ministers who in
their hearts are sick of the conflict nevertheless feel the need
to echo the tired slogans of the past—'no popery', 'no
surrender'. They fear, probably with some justification, a lay
backlash if they appear to be compromising.

Much of that backlash is fuelled by Dr Ian Paisley's Free
Presbyterian Church. It is a relatively small body (fewer than
11,000 members) but its leader is in every sense a towering
figure in the life of Northern Ireland. Those who know him
only as the Westminster MP would be surprised to hear him
in the pulpit or on the soapbox in the streets of Belfast. He
is a polemicist, a man who can play on the emotional chords
of an Ulster audience like a master organist.

His strengths are diverse. He is an Ulsterman, with a
genuine feeling for the ordinary working-class men and
women who live in the grey terraces of Belfast's Protestant
ghettoes. He is a shrewd politician, who knows how to use
his huge popular support to inhibit change, oppose reforms
or destroy opponents, as a succession of Unionist leaders have
discovered. But most of all he is a Protestant fundamentalist,
who does not hesitate to invoke a divine authority for his
words. For his followers, it is not just 'Dr Paisley's opinion'
but the word of God that proves them right and everyone
else wrong.

Paisley's political support is enormous, and extends far
beyond his own denomination. He articulates very precisely
the fears and resentments of the 'ordinary' Protestant. More
than that, he delivers the goods. If Paisley says something will
be stopped, it usually is. He has the power to make Ulster
ungovernable, and his opponents know it.

Of course, political stars can wane and circumstances
change. It is possible to construct a scenario in which Ian
Paisley loses his power base in the back streets of Belfast.
But whatever happens to him politically, the Bible-wielding
preacher will remain as an archetypal figure, the personifi-
cation of fundamentalism. The Troubles have made him a
national and even a world figure, but in any period of history
he would have made an impact on his own native environment. It is Paisley, and other lesser men like him, who have
drawn the religious map of Ulster since the settlement.

In any case, it is wrong to interpret the current religious scene in Northern Ireland solely in terms of the Troubles. It is a very 'religious' province. Most people belong to a church and many attend every week. Mission halls abound. Conventions and evangelistic meetings draw large crowds. And this is not hypocrisy, a religious veneer stuck over raw sectarian bigotry. God matters to the people of Northern Ireland, both Roman Catholic and Protestant. They say their prayers and try to love their neighbour. So far, however, they have tended to interpret 'neighbour' rather too narrowly; as the person near at hand, the member of my group, the one who is like me. Most of them will express tolerance and even affection for individual members of the other community, reserving their harshest words for the organisations that claim to represent it. They feel trapped but cannot see any way to free themselves from a situation many of them find literally intolerable.

Within Ulster Protestantism the smaller Christian groups do better than merely survive. Several are growing: notably the House Church movement and the Pentecostalists. There are relatively few Methodists (21,000) and Baptists (8,000). Indeed, the Christian Brethren, at 10,000, outnumber the Baptists. It is probable that the numbers attending various mission halls, the YMCA services and other non-denominational gatherings are quite significant.

Of course, as statistics they are insignificant when compared with the 350,000 Roman Catholics. Some 16 per cent of all Roman Catholics in the UK live in Northern Ireland. The Church is confident, traditional, authoritarian, still opposed to 'mixed company keeping' (ie Catholic boys going out with Protestant girls) and mixed marriages. Yet it includes a number of prophetic figures, priests who have identified with the poor—like the angry Fr Des Wilson—or who have argued for a more open approach to Protestants. Bishop Edward Daly of Derry is probably one of the most outstanding Roman Catholic bishops in the United Kingdom: a brave, eloquent and honest man. But the Church as a whole is a mirror image of its Protestant opposite, fostering not just a religious commitment but a total culture; not just Mass and the Angelus but Gaelic football and Republican songs. Its schools, which virtually every Roman Catholic child attends, are bastions of the social divide. Their presence and success ensure that the State schools are in fact Protestant schools. As a result, many children in Northern Ireland grow up without a single acquaintance, let alone friend, from the 'other' community. They play different games, wear different tee-shirts, sing different songs, support different football clubs. It is a bizarre situation. It will take a quality of leadership and a kind of raw courage no one has yet revealed to change it. Part of the tragedy is that it should happen to the people of this lovely province, a people steeped in the Christianity of their forefathers, a warm and friendly people who are the victims rather than the architects of their tragic situation.

In any future scenario for the Church in the United Kingdom the Christian communities in the Celtic lands will play an important role. It is no use thinking (as many do) of Church unity as the Anglicans and Catholics getting together—unless the situation in Wales, Scotland and Ulster is to be ignored. On the philosophical front, the broad-minded, religiously vague English do not approach the question of unity in the same way as the argumentative Welsh, the doctrinaire Scots or the suspicious Northern Irish. I would suggest that a unity based on English indifferentism would have very little appeal to the rest of the United Kingdom, and little likelihood of long-term success, either. The English may not welcome it, but they need to listen to and learn from their sister Churches across the borders.

CHAPTER TWELVE

CHURCHES OF THE INCOMERS

NYONE WHO CAN REMEMBER, AS I CAN, the
Britain of the immediate post-war period will realise
how remarkably the ethnic mix of the nation has
changed over the last forty years. Successive waves
of immigration, from the Caribbean, Pakistan (as it became)
and India, Cyprus and East Africa have not only changed

Afro-Caribbean Churches, 1985*

	Members	Ministers†	Churches
African Churches	10,420	1,101	104
West Indian Churches	54,904	3,091	855
Totals	65,324	4,192	959

* These figures are the official ones and do not represent actual church attendance—
 perhaps five times greater in some cases.
† Includes many part-time ministers.

Orthodox Churches, 1985

	Members*	Ministers	Churches
Greek Orthodox	101,515	99	75
Russian Orthodox	2,800	14	31
Other Orthodox	12,386	46	72
Totals	116,701	159	178

* These figures are estimates of *active* memberships. The Greek Orthodox
 Community as a whole (for example) is over 250,000.

the racial composition of the British people, but also the religious scene. Other kinds of Christianity and other religions have established themselves in a society that was previously fairly insular and prided itself on its 'Britishness'.

AFRO-CARIBBEAN CHURCHES

The immigrants from the West Indies began to arrive in the 1950s, many of them in response to recruiting campaigns by British industry and the Health Service. They brought with them a Christianity they had learned largely from British missionaries. Many were Anglicans, Roman Catholics or Methodists. But others came with one or other of the indigenous variations on traditional Christianity, mostly of a pentecostal or adventist kind.

The English (for it was mostly to the great English cities that they came) were unsure how to react to the West Indians. There was some racial rioting in West London and a good deal of tension in the run-down urban areas where most of them settled. British Christians were asked questions they did not want to answer. Were they prepared to welcome the newcomers to their Churches and—more disturbingly— adapt their worship and activities to make them feel at home? The answers to these questions were a qualified 'yes' to the first and usually an unqualified 'no' to the second, at any rate where the traditional Churches were concerned. English church worship and English Christians seemed remarkably cool and austere to most Caribbeans. Some bravely stuck it and eventually discovered that the natives were not universally unfriendly. They and their children are to found today in many inner-city churches, and increasingly some suburban ones. Many, however, simply could not find a home in the traditional Churches and gradually either opted out of church-going completely or moved into the Black-led Churches which began to plant themselves in church halls and disused chapels.

Of course, some churches *did* welcome the newcomers and reaped the benefit. I think of a handful of Anglican, Roman Catholic and Free Church congregations which went out of their way to make West Indians feel at home. Today they have predominantly black congregations, sometimes black clergy, and well-developed links with the community. There were also some evangelical Churches, mostly pentecostal or Christian Brethren, that welcomed the newcomers who felt at ease in a familiar environment.

But for the most part congregations felt they had done their duty if they allowed 'our West Indian friends' to use the church hall for worship 'in their customary exuberant style'. It is not surprising that in due course these groups moved further and further away from the mainstream Churches, eventually forming distinct congregations and even denominations. By the late 1970s these new groups were so numerous, influential and self-confident that they could begin to re-establish relationships with the older churches on terms of parity. Some joined the British Council of Churches, others the Evangelical Alliance. At the same time the older Churches, with some sense of repentance for past mistakes, recognised and accepted the Black-led Churches as an important and growing part of the British Christian scene.

However, they have been slower to recognise fully the role of black Christians in the mainline denominations. It is hard to acquire reliable statistics, but there is no doubt that the substantial numbers of black people in the congregations are nowhere near represented by their numbers in positions of leadership, whether as deacons, elders, ministers or bishops. The Church of England still has only one black bishop (Wilfred Wood, at Croydon) and pitifully few black clergy or ordinands in training. In 1986, when about a thousand men and women were in training for the Anglican ministry, only two were Afro-Caribbean. The situation is much the same in the main Free Churches and the Roman Catholic Church. Even the Seventh Day Adventist Church, with a predominantly black membership, has very few black ministers. It is said that black men and women do not offer themselves for training, or lack the necessary academic qualifications. The former is probably true, though the reason for it requires investigation. The latter may be true, if 'qualifications' are judged in terms of examination results and university degrees, but untrue in terms of pastoral and teaching ability, if the success of the Black-led Churches is anything to go by. At any rate Afro-Caribbean Christianity, in all its forms, is now a substantial element in the church life of Britain. There can

be no doubt that it will be increasingly influential at every
level, nor that eventually its influence will grow in the
traditional English Churches.

ORTHODOX CHURCHES

The Orthodox presence, however, is still in the period of
isolation. The wave of immigration from Cyprus in the fifties
and sixties brought large numbers of Greek Cypriots to a few
areas of Britain, mostly to North London. For a long while
they simply recreated their home communities in London,
people from certain towns or villages in Cyprus congregating
in specific streets in Harringay, Tottenham or Islington. They
kept to their own language—indeed, many of the older
women could speak no English at all. And they bought and
furnished Greek Orthodox Churches, mostly former Anglican
or Free Church buildings. Sometimes these Churches became
centres of political activity, too, relating to the various
divisions and tensions in Cyprus: between Greek and Turk,
and between pro-Greek Cypriots and the rest.

But as the younger generation grew up, these well-
established ethnic distinctives began to weaken. Greek
Cypriot youngsters took to English ways more readily than
Asian or Caribbean immigrants. Many of them spoke Greek
at home but hardly ever outside it. Part of this process of
cultural dilution involved their attitude towards the Church.
Few younger Cypriots became enthusiastic churchgoers,
though almost all attended the great Easter and Christmas
services and went through such rites of passage as baptism
and marriage in church. Like their elders, they could not
understand the ancient Greek used in the liturgy. Unlike their
elders, they were prepared to express their disapproval of
what they saw as 'long, boring and incomprehensible'
services.

I remember making a radio programme in the late 1970s
about the attitude of young Cypriots to the Church. Although
I had a Greek Cypriot producer's assistant, and plenty of
contacts with the community, we found it unbelievably difficult to find *one* teenager who could talk with any degree of
commitment or enthusiasm about the Orthodox faith. Most

of them felt a loyalty to the community and, as part of that, to the Church. They respected the community traditions about things like dating, arranged marriages and the extended family, even though they questioned them. But their ignorance of the actual teachings of their Church, or of the meaning of the liturgy or ritual, was almost total. This alienation of the younger generation—people who were born and have grown up in Britain—is undoubtedly the main problem facing the Greek Orthodox Church here. Some priests are not only aware of it but are trying to do something about it. On the success or failure of their efforts will depend the long-term future of the Church in Britain.

Greek Orthodox—mainly Cypriots—are by far the greater part of the Orthodox community in England—over 250,000 out of a total of about 400,000. They form the Archdiocese of Thyateira and Great Britain. The remaining 15,000 Orthodox are divided between no less than fifteen other juris-dictions, most with fewer than a thousand members. Most simply relate to different ethnic origins (Bulgarian, Estonian, Polish, Serbian and so on) though there are three Russian hierarchies, reflecting the political history of the Russian Church. There have been a number of conversions to the Orthodox faith, mostly to the Russian Orthodox Church, but it remains largely a closed book to most British Christians. That is sad, given the enormous influence the Eastern Church has had in the evolution of the faith. In recent years Orthodox Church leaders in Britain have begun to take a more active role in ecumenical affairs.

OTHER FAITHS

Apart from small groups of Asian Christians, the Afro-Carib-bean community and the people of Cypriot background make up the largest Christian element among the post-war incomers. Most of the rest are Hindus, Muslims and Sikhs, and their presence—mainly again in London and the big provincial cities—has begun to affect the religious scene in Britain very profoundly. Unlike the Jews, who have been part of our society for almost a thousand years and also share the same religious origins as the Christians, the other groups are

very sensitive about the dominant Christian culture (as they
see it) of Britain. Their main concern, understandably, is to
defend their culture against creeping assimilation. The Hindus
have probably been least successful, and the Muslims most
successful at this.

The Muslims are unique in one respect. Unlike Hindus,
Jews or Sikhs, they actually wish to win non-Muslims to their
faith. This missionary emphasis is almost totally lacking from
those religions which are basically ethnic. It makes relationships between Christians and Muslims rather more sensitive
than they are with other faiths—and this despite the fact
that theologically Christians and Muslims are far closer than
Christians and Hindus or Sikhs.

The presence of the other faiths has kept the issue of multi-
faith education and inter-faith activity to the fore. It is
generally accepted now that religious education should be
multi-faith, introducing pupils to the beliefs and practices of
all the world's major religions, while giving rather more time,
of course, to the Christianity which has shaped the culture
and ethic of Britain. Even denominational church schools, by
and large, include a study of comparative religion in their
syllabuses.

Multi-faith education has its problems, though. There is
clearly a danger that children will grow up with a phenomeno-
logical approach to religion, without any experience of it as
a way of life that involves commitment. They will know that
Hindus reverence the cow, that Muslims go on pilgrimage
to Mecca, that Sikhs have a Golden Temple and Jews Ten
Commandments. But religion is much more than its outward
observances. It is a thing of the head and the heart and
can only truly be understood from *within*. Those who are
committed to their own faith, experiencing it as it were from
the inside, are much better placed to respect and even understand someone else's religion. It is at least arguable that children should be introduced to the faith of their own
community in a profound way *before* being exposed to the
religious supermarket which is modern Britain.

The major faiths are represented on many advisory bodies,
including broadcasting ones, and their leaders are gradually
building bridges of mutual respect with their opposite
numbers in the Christian Churches. It will take a long while,

I imagine, before it reaches the degree of warmth with which the Chief Rabbi is regarded by church leaders, but that is the direction in which it should go. My own conviction is that respect for the faith, culture and traditions of others is an essential element in the building of a sound multi-faith society, but that such respect does not demand compromise over one's beliefs. I do not expect a Muslim to deny that Islam is a unique revelation of God to the human race. Equally, I do not expect to be inhibited from saying that Jesus Christ is the unique way to God: 'No one comes to the Father except through him.' Mutual respect means what it says: the dictionary calls it 'reverential esteem'. I should value my fellow citizens' beliefs and treat them with reverence. That does not mean that I may not think them wrong, nor be denied the right to say so. Equally I must not deny that right to them.

All of this is relevant to the vexed question of inter-faith services. The most notable in recent years, I imagine, was a great celebration of the earth at Assisi in 1987, when Christians, Jews, Muslims, Hindus, Buddhists and others joined in a service of prayer for the environment. The world's religious leaders were there, including the Pope, and many distinguished statesmen and public figures, including the Duke of Edinburgh. The service was full of appeals to the 'religious spirit we all share' and prayers were offered to the assortment of deities represented by the participants. It was a version on the grand scale of the kind of smaller events that are often attempted locally. I have to say that like those, it left me cold.

I work with people of all faiths, sit on committees and boards with them, and live in a multi-cultural area of London. I am as committed as anyone could be to the need to build a genuinely multi-cultural society in Britain. I believe that an essential part of that, as I have said, is mutual respect for each others' religious beliefs. But I cannot see that I am expressing 'respect' or 'reverence' for another man's beliefs if in doing so I am denying or compromising my own. I would not ask him to deny or compromise *his* beliefs to accommodate mine; and if I did I should be undermining the whole concept of mutual respect.

So, for me, a service where a Hindu reads the poems of Rabindranath Tagore, a Muslim recites the Qur'an, a Sikh

chants from the Grant Sahib and a Christian declaims the
Beatitudes, does not advance the cause of mutual respect. It
implies what is manifestly untrue, namely, that there is some
core of common faith here: 'After all, we all worship the
same God'. Of course, we do not. Buddhists do not worship
an infinite personal God who objectively exists outside and
beyond his creatures. The Hindu God expresses divinity in a
thousand forms; the Christian God in a Trinity of Persons.
We do not serve truth well when we deliberately blur its
edges. Part of true respect is respecting differences, and inter-
faith 'services' fail to do that.

Whether such services become more common or not—and
my impression is that their heyday was in the 1970s—there
is no doubt that the Christian Churches are going to have to
think very hard about their approach to the other faiths.
Some Christians feel our overwhelming responsibility is to
share with them the good news of Christ: what they call
evangelism and the other faiths call proselytism. Other Christians believe we should engage in dialogue, finding common
ground and making common cause whenever we can. Yet
other Christians simply never give a second thought to the
millions of their fellow countrymen who follow these great
and ancient faiths. Whether we see their presence as a mission
field on our doorstep, or a treasure store of spiritual variety
to be explored, it seems stupid to ignore them. Out-and-out
direct evangelism is likely to threaten the stability of our
fragile communal peace in Britain's great cities, but some
combination of genuine interest, respect and friendliness with
a patient attempt to share the Christian gospel seems to be
the most profitable response. What Christians cannot do is
close their eyes to the situation. It is too near, too big and
too important for that.

CHAPTER THIRTEEN

THE CHURCHES AND THE MEDIA

T HE ADVENT OF THE 'MODERN' MEDIA OF
RADIO AND TELEVISION more or less coincided
with the beginning of the present phase of decline
in religious observance. It is tempting to see this as
a simple matter of cause and effect. Along comes radio and
then television, to provide entertainment on tap, day and
night; and out goes churchgoing. After all, who would take
the trouble to go out to a cold, cheerless, uninviting service
when a touch on a switch can bring the Church—and much
else besides—into your own lounge?

It is tempting to make the connection, and ever since public
radio broadcasting began in 1922 some Christians have done
so. The *Methodist Recorder* warned that the advent of the
'wireless' would inevitably undermine churchgoing. When
television made its great advance in the early 1950s there was
no shortage of clerics to warn that it would spell the end of
civilisation as we had known it—no more fireside conver-
sations, no more singsongs around the piano, no more family
prayers . . . and no more regular churchgoing.

It is true, of course, that television, especially, has made
any activity outside the home less attractive. Not only the
churches, but also the theatre, the cinema and sports arenas
have found it much harder to attract regular audiences. The
decline in cinema attendance has been far greater than the
decline in churchgoing, for instance. But just as the home
video has maintained the popularity of the film, and televised
sport has kept the population sports-conscious, so radio and

television have brought religious ideas and worship into the homes of Britain to an extent that is probably unprecedented in the Christian era.

Not surprisingly, therefore, the relationship between the Churches and the broadcasters has often been somewhat fraught. At first the Churches were suspicious of broadcasting, seeing it as a dangerous rival. Then they changed their attitude, recognising its enormous influence, and tried to enlist it as an ally. Today there is a division of opinion. Some church leaders still see television and radio in its public service guise as an important means of Christian communication, fundamentally 'on the side of the angels', while others regard it rather as a tool of the devil, advocating immoral and anti-social attitudes and portraying a religion of doubt and division.

There is little doubt that television is a catalyst of social change, if only because it brings new ideas, styles and attitudes to a wide public at great speed. In that sense, it has been an important element in the vast shift of social and moral attitudes in the last thirty years. Ideas that were hitherto more or less confined to an exotic 'elite' in Kensington and Hampstead have become popular property, especially through television drama. Television did not invent the live-in lover, but it has helped to make the idea 'respectable'. Adultery predates the television age by many millenia, but never before have so many people had so many examples of it displayed alluringly before them. An avid viewer of television drama in the sixties and seventies who was living a celibate or monogamous life far from West London must have felt a distinct oddity. One has some sympathy with the man who is alleged to have phoned Directory Enquiries for the number of the Permissive Society, as he wanted to join it.

The answer of the broadcasting chiefs to the allegation that they have connived at the break-up of national morality is that their programmes have reflected changes in society, rather than causing them. Thus (in this argument) a more casual attitude to extra-marital sex, a benevolent view of homosexuality and a general loosening up in the area of what might be called 'bad language' *preceded* the widespread portrayal of such things on the television screen. Broadcasting simply reflected what was already happening in society.

There is, of course, some truth in this. But even to reflect something is, in a sense, to promote it. If I reflect a beam of light, I multiply it and diversify its effect. And that, I believe, is what television did in the sixties and seventies. It reflected an actual trend, most noticeable in the big cities and especially, perhaps, in the narrow world inhabited by television writers and directors, and in doing so multiplied and diversified it. My imaginary monogamous citizen of Sheffield was suddenly faced with the morality of London's media set, day after day, until it seemed like normality.

I do not think any neutral observer could deny that there was a deliberate campaign in the sixties by some writers and directors to bring about a change in our society's moral attitudes. In the words of Roy Jenkins (Home Secretary for part of this period), it was the 'civilised' rather than the 'permissive' society which they thought they were bringing in: but their notion of 'civilisation' amounted to the endorsement of 'permissive' attitudes: in practice the two aims tended to be identical. Those who set out to liberate people from what they regarded as the straitjacket of Victorian morality can hardly have guessed what a Pandora's box they were opening. Marriage faced a two-pronged onslaught, from those feminists who saw it as bondage for women, and from those men who wanted to justify promiscuity, or at any rate the idea of plural partners. The divorce rate soared and the broken home became commonplace. The strong existentialism of much drama of the sixties and seventies emphasised experience. There was a distinct air of hedonism about— enjoy yourself, make the most of your opportunities, follow your instincts. Overshadowing much of this period as well was the Vietnam War, with its constant risk of escalation to global conflict. When a mood of insecurity (especially among the young) coincides with a period of economic affluence, hedonism is a predictable consequence. And so it was.

Whether the broadcasters *could* have held the line against the so-called new morality I do not know. I suspect it was impossible. But in any case there was a reluctance on their part to be cast in the Reithian role of defenders of the nation's morals. Under Hugh Carleton Greene, most notably, the BBC embraced the general mood of liberalisation. Most people remember from that period the political satire of *That Was the Week That Was*, but probably even more influential was the *Wednesday Play*, drip-feeding progressive ideas into six million sitting rooms every week. Britain *did* change its moral stance during this period, whatever the means by which this change was brought about, and it would be a rash observer who claimed that television had nothing, or little, to do with it. And it was this period that began to see the break-up of the unwritten coalition between the Churches and the broadcasters.

This came about in various ways. At the simplest level, the shift towards a greater liberty for the programme-makers meant, almost inevitably, the broadcasting of much more material offensive to the religious minority in society. What was worse, when they wrote to the Director-General or the Chairman of the BBC to complain, they received unsympathetic replies. Apparently the old argument—that this was a Christian country, and that it was the BBC's duty to maintain Christian standards—no longer carried much weight. Popular public opinion was cited to refute it. Thirty-five million people watched *Till Death Us Do Part* each week, despite its coarse language and crude attitudes ... or, perhaps, *because* of them. Church people, even clergy and bishops, found that they were treated like a slightly eccentric minority pressure group rather than as the accepted guardians of the nation's conscience. Their letters might appear in *The Times*—and even, occasionally, the *Radio Times*—but they were unable to influence the policy of the broadcasters. I think it was at this period that many Christians decided to stop thinking of the BBC (especially) as an ally and instead to regard it as either neutral or even an enemy of the gospel.

But the coalition was damaged in other and more subtle ways. The Epilogue more or less disappeared from our screens, though it took twenty years for some comedians to realise it had gone. Somehow it seems symptomatic of all the other changes. For a decade and more after World War II the BBC, and then ITV in its turn, felt it appropriate that the last programme of the day should be a religious reflection, followed, naturally, by the national anthem. So at some witching hour a nervous cleric would smile at a single camera in a tiny studio somewhere and deliver himself of a homily— which was heard, one imagines, by a solid core of insomniacs.

It was a nod to God, I know: but it reflected, if only in a token way, the assumption that religion, and specifically the Christian faith, was part of the broadcasting establishment. 'They' felt it should be there, really whether anyone wanted it or not. It was right and proper.

The Epilogue's disappearance (except in a few regional ITV stations) must be seen in the context of a total change of policy in religious broadcasting: a change welcomed by some church leaders, but bitterly resented and resisted by others, and probably by a majority of ordinary churchgoers. Since a series of talks by an atheist philosopher, Dr Margaret White, on the Home Service in the early 1950s, which argued that belief in God is not essential for morality, the BBC has occasionally risked the ire of the godly with broadcasts of controversial material critical of the Christian position. But this was nothing compared to the positive flood of such ideas in the sixties and seventies—not all of it, by any means, in the output of the Religious Broadcasting Department. Major television series like *The Ascent of Man*, by Professor Julian Bronowski and *The Long Search* by Ronald Eyre challenged the traditional concepts of Christianity root and branch. For them, belief in a Creator (in the first case) or in a specific revelation through prophets, Christ and Bible (in the second) were no more than possible—and, it seemed, rather unlikely—options. Again, many church people were scandalised. But Magnus Magnusson's series on biblical archeology and Don Cupitt's sceptical investigation of the life and teaching of Jesus came in their wake, as though the protests had never been made. The point was being hammered home that the Churches and their beliefs were simply on a par with many other possible interpretations of truth. They no longer had exclusive or unique access to those areas of broadcasting where religious ideas were being considered.

This change in broadcasting policy towards religion was, of course, part of the far greater change that we have seen in broadcasting as a whole. The Central Religious Advisory Committee (known internally by the rather odd acronym CRAC), which advises both the BBC and the IBA on religious broadcasting policy, was chaired during the critical years by Robert Runcie, then Bishop of St Albans and later, of course, Archbishop of Canterbury. He recalls with some satisfaction the task to which they set themselves at that time: to lay down guidelines for a new kind of approach to religious broadcasting, in which that tacit coalition of Church and broadcasters was abandoned in favour of a more open policy, which would reflect the new situation in Britain.

This would have several ramifications. The old 'closed period', when BBC and ITV conspired to force the early Sunday evening viewer to watch religion whether he liked it or not, would have to go. Religious television would have to follow the example of religious radio and compete for time on the air on merit. No one knew what the consequences of this decision would be. Many feared the worst: the total disappearance of the audience and hence, eventually, the total disappearance of religious programmes too.

Then, the presence in Britain of substantial minorities who followed other religious faiths needed to be recognised. For the first time a Muslim was invited to join CRAC, and an effort was begun to involve the non-Christian faiths in religious programmes on radio and television. The significance of this for policy was that it underlined the disappearance of the old equation: religious broadcasting equals Christian propaganda. The new CRAC guidelines proposed that the output should be 'mainly though not exclusively Christian', but went on to make it clear that yet another group of people was also to be considered: 'those outside, or on the fringe of, the organised life of the churches'. In other words, programmes were no longer to be made simply for Christians, or on the assumption that all listeners to the BBC were implicitly, if not explicitly, Christians. Programmes should involve the whole debate about ultimate meaning and reality, everything encompassed by the phrase 'the religious dimension of life'. It was a charter for exploration rather than proclamation, and so it has proved.

The 1980s have demonstrated the wisdom of those decisions. In a multi-faith society, in which there are many different groups of highly committed believers, but in the context of a generally agnostic majority, the new policy was the only one likely to be sustainable by a public corporation like the BBC or a commercial enterprise like ITV. It did not and does not mean that there is no room in the output for the direct proclamation of a religious message. The Churches are still, in effect, 'given' hundreds of hours every year of broadcasting time within which they have almost total freedom to put across their message. I am thinking of broadcast services and talks. But for the rest of the output—the features and documentaries, the magazine programmes and discussions—the BBC and the IBA have no credal stance to sustain nor any coalition or covert agreement with the Churches to fulfil. The air is free. A thousand thoughts contend. To those of us who believe that 'great is the truth and will prevail' this is not a disaster but an exciting opportunity.

In the event, the changes consequent upon the abandoning of the 'closed period' did not spell the end of religious broadcasting. Quite the reverse. The BBC's major religious documentary effort was shifted from early Sunday evening, when it was too indigestible for family viewing, to a strand after the late evening news. There *Anno Domini* and its successor *Everyman*, and *Heart of the Matter*, which alternates with it, have attracted substantial audiences, on a par with those for the major current affairs, science and arts documentaries. *Credo* and *Seven Days* on ITV have also flourished in the new freedom of placing. At the same time in the old 'God-slot' *Songs of Praise* (BBC) and *Highway* (ITV) slug it out, each attracting something over seven million viewers in competition with the ungodly fare on the other two channels. Each of them comfortably attracts a bigger audience than *Match of the Day*. It may be fortunate, or providential, that the upsurge in interest in religion which I noted in an earlier chapter more or less coincided with the shift in policy. Certainly radio and television audiences for religious programmes are buoyant—both for those of an exploratory kind, and for the more committed kind of broadcasting.

In general the Churches have come to accept their new relationship with the broadcasters, just as they have come to accept a new role in a multi-faith and agnostic society. Undoubtedly some Church leaders and many ordinary Christians deplore the way things have gone, and recall nostalgically the 'old days' when the BBC was in effect a mouthpiece for Christianity (or at any rate one kind of uncontroversial Christianity). But realistically they know that this is the best they can expect in the present broadcasting situation—a generous share in an open public platform.

However, the present broadcasting situation is a highly temporary phenomenon. New technology and a government committed to the free play of the market have created a set of conditions which are ripe for exploitation. In any case direct broadcasting by satellite (DBS) makes almost any notion of governmental or corporate 'control' of programmes impossible. Once the satellite dish is in position, any one can choose his own programme from the range of material being beamed at his region. By the 1990s that will certainly include at least half a dozen European-based and American channels. Our existing four channels (which may by then be five, or even more) will be in direct competition with free (ie advertisement-bearing), sponsored and subscription programmes from many parts of the world. Broadcasting in Britain, which has been so neat and tidy for nearly seventy years, will become a hectic free-for-all.

Will the BBC, in anything like its present guise, survive all this? And will religious broadcasting as we have known it— that is to say, open, balanced, moderate and responsible output—survive as well? I have no doubt that the highly aggressive, didactic, persuasive and at times polemic programmes of the American electronic church will be there, competing for attention and funds. It is quite probable that one or more of a score of British-based bodies who are itching to provide similar but more indigenous fare will also have acquired access to our screens.

The situation may be not unlike that facing the newspaper world with the proliferation of free papers. Generally speaking they have successfully coped with the new situation, some by going down-market and staking everything on soft porn, sport and bingo, and others by going up-market and offering ever thicker papers with ever more substantial features and coverage. Both, in their very distinct ways, have increased their sales, even though the free sheets have flourished all over the country. Probably more papers are being read—if only for the advertisements—than ever before in the history of Britain.

In other words multiplication of new outlets does not necessarily lead to the extermination of the original ones. It may be that public service broadcasting in its BBC form— and even perhaps, in its IBA model—can not only survive but flourish in the brave new world of communication technology. Possibly the new outlets, like the free papers, will gain access to most homes without completely ousting the old ones. It may be that the British public, who by general consent have been served rather better than most nations by their broadcasters, will prove more selective than viewers in other lands. Perhaps they will reject as rubbish the material coming 'free' from people whose main motive is to enlist or exploit them.

There is a specific problem facing the Christian Churches here, and it is likely that different groups will come to widely differing conclusions about it. How much effort and resources should they put into the alternative forms of broadcasting? In effect they have had coverage of religious affairs, discussions of religious topics and the broadcasting of Christian worship free of charge for over sixty years. It may be difficult for Churches which have become used to extensive religious programming funded by the licence fee to accustom themselves to the need to buy time and pay for programmes. But that may be the price of effective competition in the free-for-all that most experts predict. The alternative is to give fringe groups, mavericks and religious entrepreneurs, British or American, a free run of the available channels.

As so often, the transatlantic precedent is important. The major denominations in the United States kept aloof from the electronic church in its early stages, at first ignoring and then denouncing its excesses, while relying on the big networks to maintain their traditional coverage of religious affairs and activities. What in fact happened was that the electronic church advanced steadily: not in size of audience, but in multiplicity of outlets. Eventually there were 'specialist' channels in every area of the USA, offering day-long wall-to-wall religion, usually of a fundamentalist kind, with an eclectic audience of the already committed, whose free-will gifts kept the stations on the air. At the same time, the response of the major networks was to reduce their coverage of religion. After all, there was 'religion', of a kind, available on tap everywhere in the nation. Consequently the mainline denominations were left stranded, ostracised and frequently denounced by the tele-evangelists, and abandoned by the networks, without any significant platform for their beliefs and certainly not one commensurate with their size. As a result they came late in the day to accept the idea of 'paid-for' programming—late, but sometimes, especially in the case of the Roman Catholics, very effectively.

In Britain the pattern is likely to be similar. I should expect most of the religion on the alternative channels—DBS (Direct Broadcasting by Satellite) or cable—to come either from established American sources like CBN (Christian Broadcasting Network) or from British counterparts probably funded by various evangelical groups, especially the House Churches. As in America, this will vary from very good of its kind to appalling, and from religio-political posturing to straight evangelistic preaching. Little of it, on present evidence, would be very sympathetic towards the established Churches, and much of it would be condemnatory.

The Churches seem to have two possible courses of action: to create their own broadcasting production houses, and compete with the electronic church from the word go; or to trust that public service broadcasting, in one or other model, will continue to flourish and to provide space for the serious consideration of religious issues and for Christian worship and proclamation. The first would be very costly—a million pounds could disappear in a matter of weeks. The second would be rather risky, if we take the American precedent seriously, but may yet be the wiser option.

However, there is another possible course of action, I believe, and it is one which I hope the various mainline Churches will take seriously. It is a kind of midway option, which would enable the Churches to take full advantage of the opportunities provided by public service broadcasting, while equipping themselves to respond positively and effectively if that outlet were denied to them or drastically diminished. The larger denominations already have embryonic broadcasting wings, often staffed by able men and women with substantial media experience. At present they advise, train, liaise with broadcasting outlets, provide research and information and make the occasional educational or promotional videotape. Their budgets are small, and their role is probably undervalued by most of the denominational hierarchies.

The new situation ought to change that. Communication

is at the very heart of Christianity. The apostle Paul made use of every possible medium of communication available to him: from the market place to the intellectual forum (see Acts 17:16ff). It seems unlikely that if he were around today he would have ignored such splendid platforms for his message as radio and television. Yet the media departments of the Churches are still the poor relations. Ordination training, the care of church buildings, even the upkeep of episcopal palaces, receive a vastly greater share of the Church of England's resources, and it is much the same in the other denominations. If effective involvement in broadcasting were to be put on a par with these other, admittedly vital, demands on the Church's purse, the position would be transformed. With the BBC committed to taking a substantial part of its output from independent producers, and with an explosion of demand imminent with the multiplication of outlets, seed-money for production could be effectively used. Not only that, but the potential would exist to move into the commercial DBS and cable field if that proved necessary—not as a poor relation, but with proven skills and expertise. The Roman Catholics in the United States have shown what can be done, not by throwing vast sums of money into speculative productions, but by encouraging talent, providing facilities and training participants. It is a belt-and-braces option, of course; quite unnecessary if the present level of religious broadcasting continues, with satisfactory audiences, into the 1990s. Yet it seems to me only prudent to make plans that can cope with either scenario: one in which the BBC and ITV continue to dominate the television scene, and the alternative one in which the multiplication of outlets marginalises the output of the present networks and creates a new, popular broadcasting medium, available via satellite and generally free of charge.

I have written of the change that happened in religious broadcasting a decade or more ago, and of the changes that seem to await us a decade or less ahead. Paradoxically, the present is a period of conservatism in society generally and also in religion, and this is reflected in broadcasting output as well as in public attitudes. After the licence of the sixties and early seventies, the pendulum has swung emphatically. Perhaps proving that the BBC *does* reflect rather than create standards, programmes are more cautious now, less iconoclastic and stridently shocking than they were ten or twenty years ago. There is no political satire on BBC television now to match *That Was the Week*, no irreverent humour to match *Monty Python*, no speculative theology to match Cupitt's *Jesus* programmes. Cupitt's *Sea of Faith* (1985) was certainly unorthodox, but it had been a long while in the making, and I do not expect it will have many successors in the near future.

Not only that, but every BBC executive knows the ferocity of the campaign against blasphemy, indecency and obscenity. The volume of apparently spontaneous complaint is higher now than in the recent past—an odd phenomenon, because the daring young men and women of the fifties are now the middle-aged protesters against the erosion of standards. This, in turn, may be a passing thing, and broadcasters cannot create a policy for the future on the shifting sand of public moods. But that very shift is a warning that there is no irreversible or irresistible movement of history moving relentlessly towards some liberal 'golden' age. Opinion can move to the right as well as to the left. People can look nostalgically to the past as well as longingly to the future. In other words, no battle for public opinion is ever finally won or lost. In the bright new media world that beckons us, it is worth remembering that.

CHAPTER FOURTEEN

A MATTER OF IMAGES

IT IS HARD TO REMEMBER NOW THE DAYS when image simply did not matter. Prime Ministers like Clement Attlee could be as anonymous as they liked. Archbishops could be pompous and boring. Food could be sold in plain paper bags. Political parties had public policies rather than public relations. No one would be rejected for the highest office in the land because he looked too posh on television. No one would lose a General Election because he wore ill-fitting anoraks.

But the age of the image has come, riding in on the back of television and supported by the press and radio. It is not only what you are, but what you seem to be that matters; not simply what you propose, but what you project. Image is how things are seen rather than how they really are, but because it affects people's reactions and responses it is not easily dismissed. For a long while the Churches professed to despise image, but eventually—reluctantly, perhaps—they too began to worry about it. They eventually came to believe that it is not enough to hold the truth. It must be presented (packaged, or projected) in a way that will attract attention and command a response. That, at least, is the theory.

The 1960s saw the beginning of this particular revolution. It was then that the mainline Churches realised that they were being left behind in the new age of consumer choice. The age of affluence ('You've never had it so good') ushered in the age of design, marketing and presentation. But this was uncharted territory for the Churches. Until the 1960s there were no denominational press offices or public relations officers. Even archbishops made do with the odd chaplain—sometimes, very odd. The Church press looked, for the most part, thirty years out of date. Religious books had an antiquarian feel to them. Religious broadcasting was suspect. When an Anglican clergyman joined the BBC in 1964 his bishop expressed regret that he was 'leaving the Church'. Church buildings and grounds generally presented an unwelcoming aspect: illegible notice boards, dark, poorly lit interiors, a few curling post-cards and grey parish magazines on the book table and dark paint everywhere. Carpet was as rare as cloth of gold. The whole scene shouted 'keep out'. It was a vain gesture to print a ritual 'All are Welcome' in Gothic script at the foot of the church notices. It may have been true, but it did not *seem* to be true.

As the editor at the time of a moderately progressive Christian periodical (progressive in style and presentation, at any rate) I was sharply aware of the problem. In 1961 the most heated controversy in our columns was over the retention of the King James Version of the Bible. The great fear was of gimmicks, by which many people meant religious films, guitars and drama. 'Style' was highly suspect. Billy Graham, however, had shown the value of image. His message was thoroughly traditional and conservative, but his presentation was colourful, exciting and appealing. He dressed well, decked his platform with flowers (guess what *that* lot cost!) and took every possible opportunity to use the mass media. Many Christians—not all of them stick-in-the-muds, by any means—found all of this rather brash, but they began to see that it was the price one paid in order to be heard.

Slowly the religious world learned the lesson. Image actually mattered. If the church magazine which dropped through every letter-box in the parish each month represented the Church as dowdy, ugly and out of date, then those who picked it up off the doormat would receive precisely that message. If church leaders on television looked like refugees from Barchester, then who could blame the viewing public for assuming that they had no serious contribution to make to life in the swinging sixties?

One by one the main Churches set up their press and public relations offices. So did the major missionary societies and religious movements. Slowly Christian literature was revamped. Bit by bit churches attended to their decor. Good design ceased to be 'worldly' and became 'welcoming'. Carpet made a belated appearance in church, to be rapidly followed by coffee (those who had installed brown carpet saved money on replacements). The Churches Television Centre (at Bushey in Hertfordshire) and the Catholic Radio and Television Centre (at Hatch End, in Middlesex) began to persuade bishops and clergy that radio and television were not simply tools of the devil, but media that provided bridges across the yawning gulf between ordinary people and the Churches.

The process was a slow one, and uneven. Too often a denominational press and media office was the first victim of budgetary cuts. Some denominations were more reluctant than others to see this as a proper way to spend money. In general the Free Churches, with the exception of the Methodists, were slower than the Anglicans and Roman Catholics to develop their public relations structure, and they have paid the price over the years of being frequently ignored or misrepresented by the media. But gradually the picture has improved, and both nationally and locally Churches have worked hard and effectively at improving their links with newspapers, radio and television, and creating a positive public image.

Most of this was undoubtedly good. Indeed, without it one wonders whether the Churches would have survived at all as credible contributors to our national life. But image, while a powerful ally, can also be a deceitful one. It is entirely proper to present the truth in as attractive and interesting a way as possible; it is quite improper, however, to allow the image to dictate the content. The right question is, 'What is the message we have, and how can we best convey it?' The wrong question is, 'What do the people want to hear, and how can we best give it to them?' In the eighties I fear that the Churches have at times moved dangerously near to the latter position. It is not hard to find examples, and the handling of a debate in the Church of England's General Synod in the Autumn of 1987 on the subject of sexuality is a good enough one.

The debate was initiated by an Essex vicar, Tony Higton, who had put down a private member's motion which condemned sexual immorality, and specifically homosexual activity, in strong terms. It called on the Church to discipline homosexual clergy and to reaffirm traditional biblical standards. It attracted a good deal of support from members of synod and was consequently selected for debate at the autumn sessions. As it happened (and I am persuaded that it *was* a coincidence) these sessions also saw the presentation of a church report on AIDS.

This presented the stage managers of synod with a serious problem. Obviously it was essential to keep these two issues distinct. AIDS is a topic of major news interest; so, to put it mildly, is sex, especially irregular sex. Add the ingredient of religion, and you have the ideal recipe for a Fleet Street front-page story, especially in the popular papers. The decision was taken to have the AIDS debate first, and then, two days later, take Higton's motion on sexual morality.

So far, so good. But at this point those responsible for the Church's image lost their nerve, it seems to me. Mindful of what Fleet Street might make of it, they tried to pre-empt what looked like a media field day. Any stick, of course, would do for some papers to beat the Church of England— especially a week or two after Mrs Thatcher had called on church leaders to stand up for traditional moral values. Supposing synod declined to pass Mr Higton's sternly worded motion? Then out would come the media mallet labelled 'Trendy Wets', to batter the Church for being soft on sin. But, on the other hand, supposing synod were to pass the motion, perhaps by a large majority? Why, another stick would be selected from the journalistic armoury: the one labelled 'Narrow Bigots'. This time the Church would be condemned as fanatical and uncaring (as Chief Constable Anderton was pilloried for taking much that line in public earlier in the year).

Faced with this dilemma, image and principle briefly struggled for mastery. It would not be true to say that principle perished, but it would be fair to allege that image was allowed to influence crucial decisions. As a result, after the debate the press discovered *both* sticks could be used: the Church was simultaneously—and sometimes in the same paper—attacked for being both over-tolerant *and* bigoted. The reason for the confusion was an amended motion, proposed by the Bishop of Chester, which unambiguously asserted the traditional biblical standards (sex only within monogamous marriage) but chose to use a different phrase to describe homosexual genital activity (*'falling short* of this ideal'') from the one used for other sexual misdemeanours (*'sins* against this ideal'). Now those who are well versed in New Testament theology will recognise that 'falling short of an ideal'—*hamartia*, in Greek—is one of its definitions of sin (see, for instance, Romans 3:23). However, most newspaper readers—and newspaper writers, unfortunately—were apparently not aware of this particular nuance. To them it was a fudge, a failure to call sin 'sin'. Falling short of an ideal is something we all do all the time, they argued. Just like sinning, the orthodox Christian might respond: but that is not (or does not seem to be) the same thing as an unambiguous rejection of a specific act of sin.

In the end, the Church of England unquestionably got the worst of it. Its own members, who rely largely on the national press, radio and television to tell them what has happened in synod, were given the impression that the Church's leadership had ducked the issue. They had wanted to condemn homosexual activity, especially among the clergy, but had held back from committing themselves actually to do anything about it. In the light of detailed revelations in a scurrilous piece in a Sunday newspaper, they appeared to lack the courage to act decisively. In fact, of course, subsequent events proved the Bishop of Chester and the majority of synod right and most of Fleet Street wrong: firm steps have been taken to bar practising homosexuals from public ministry in the Church. At the same time, the 'liberal' wing of public opinion was dismayed to find the Church taking so apparently unsympathetic a view of even stable homosexual relationships. In an attempt to 'manage' the news, the Church had succeeded only in making itself look mildly ridiculous—especially when both Tony Higton and the Gay Christian Movement claimed the debate and its outcome as victories!

It is always easy to be wise after the event, and I do not share the view that this debate did the Church of England irretrievable harm, any more than the overblown and ultimately tragic affair the same autumn of Dr Gareth Bennett and the Crockford's Preface. Indeed, such evidence as I can obtain suggests that attendance and communicants at

Christmas 1987, a few weeks after both events, were at a higher level than for many years. A Gallup Poll showed the Archbishop of Canterbury rising in popularity with the clergy and he even won a place for the first time in Radio 4 *Today* programme's *Man of the Year Poll*. Perhaps all of this proves the truth of that tired adage, 'There's no such thing as bad publicity'.

Fortunately for the Church, many people saw behind the attempted media manipulation and the actual media distortion to a body engaged in an honest, agonised and painful argument with itself over a major issue of morality. The debate itself was splendid, as synod debates often are: courteous but sharp, thoughtful, intelligent and sensitive. And the outcome, for all the confusion it may have caused, reflected precisely those qualities. Synod did not want to start a witch hunt. It was not in the business of casting the first stone. But it did want to affirm its loyalty to traditional Christian morality. The drafting of the amended motion might have been done more carefully; the press might have been better briefed on its meaning. But in the end the truth was revealed: not a nice, clean, black-and-white truth packaged for headline writers, but a painful, tense, give-and-take truth that cannot be conveyed in slogans. The image of the Church may have suffered temporarily, but no harm at all was done to the image of the gospel.

I said that I feared the Church had at times veered towards the attitude that presenting a good image meant giving the public what it wanted, and that the sexuality debate was a good example of it. That is not to say that I believe that anyone consciously set out to ask 'What do people want to hear us say about homosexual practice?' Instead, I think there was a media-induced fear of what might happen if the General Synod were given its head simply to debate the issue and vote on it: a fear of what the papers might make of the resulting confusion. The Church House press staff are able journalists: they knew the likely outcome. So did the agenda committee and the bishops. Out of anxiety, I believe, they tried to devise a formula that would pre-empt criticism from both sides. But for once I think the proper response would have been to ignore the possible press reaction, have the debate—warts and all—and risk letting people see that there is no single hold-all position over such complex issues in the Church. Instead there was a desperate search for a form of words which might satisfy everybody, or almost everybody, and keep the press quiet. It was not a compromise, because the motion eventually passed was in principle totally uncompromising. But it had built-in ambiguities, or expressions that were capable of being taken as ambiguous, and it was that very flaw, that 'falling short of an ideal', that created the media confusion.

To be effective, in any Christian sense, image must reflect reality: it must be true to itself. The strength of Pope John-Paul II, for instance, is his unswerving consistency. He comes across as warm, open-hearted, committed and courageous: basically a likable man, someone you would enjoy meeting. The fact that he is also stubborn, conservative and single-minded does not contradict that image, but complements it. No one has to sell the Pope as a born leader: he clearly *is* a born leader.

The Churches in modern Britain are rightly conscious of their need to project a good image, as friendly, caring communities with a message relevant to today. Consequently nowadays they try to see that their plant and premises, their decor and furnishings, their notice boards and news sheets, their publicity in the local press and their day-to-day public contacts reflect that caring and relevant image. That is good, and it has no doubt contributed to the improvement of the Church's image. The problem arises when and if that image runs into conflict with some vital aspect of the Church's message—perhaps an unpopular stand over an issue of public morality or church discipline. If the choice is between faithfulness to the gospel or public approval, then there can be no hesitation in making the decision. The early Church began with a good public image: 'enjoying the favour of all the people' (Acts 2:47). It became even better: 'they were highly regarded by the people' (Acts 5:13). Yet very quickly this changed to bitter resentment and hatred: 'a great persecution broke out against the church in Jerusalem' (Acts 8:1). Their message had not changed, nor had their activities or their presentation of that message. What had changed was that very fickle thing: public opinion. Image-building, in its professional sense, is the attempt to manage public opinion, but it is inevitably an inexact science: as I have said, a powerful but potentially treacherous ally. The Churches of Britain have learnt a great deal about image since the early 1960s, and that is good. But they must resist the temptation to treat it with too much respect. Sometimes public approval is a good thing: 'all spoke well of him', as Luke writes of Jesus at Nazareth (Lk 4:22). Yet that public approval can evaporate overnight. The same people a few minutes later tried to throw Jesus over a cliff (Lk 4:29). Perhaps the Church's image-makers might have written in letters of gold above their word processors some other words of Jesus: 'Woe to you when all men speak well of you' (Lk 6:26).

CHAPTER FIFTEEN

WHO'S FOR CHURCH?

I F THERE IS ONE THING MORE THAN ANY OTHER
that I have learned from my seventeen years in religious
broadcasting, it is that Christianity in Britain amounts
to much more than the sum total of churchgoing. And
that, I suppose, has been the one underlying theme of this
book. Modern Britain is not, by and large, a churchgoing
society, but it is very far from being a secular one. The 'Great
Church of the Unchurched' (the phrase is Gerald Priestland's
invention) is real and almost certainly growing. The vast
majority of British people say they believe in God, and it is
sectarianism of the worst kind that dismisses such a claim as
meaningless.

All the same, churchgoing and church membership *are*
important. They are important as signs of commitment, as
marks of the presence of the kingdom and—more
prosaically—as the only practical means of ensuring the economic viability of the Churches. If no one belonged and no one
went to church, then the entire visible structure of Christianity
would disappear. There would be no clergy, no church buildings, no public acts of worship, no sacraments and ordinances
available for people who wished to mark the rites of passage
in life. Even if one thinks of churchgoing and membership in
terms of basic communities or house churches, attendance
and membership are vital elements. Nothing, certainly no
movement of faith or ideas, can prosper unless enough people
feel totally committed to it.

So it is not unreasonable of the Churches to think about

increasing church attendance and membership. They are rightly unhappy about the steady decline in both which occurred throughout the forty years or so following World War I. Indeed, if the trend had continued, that dreadful prospect would have arisen: the disappearance of the visible Church from our society. In fact, as we have seen, the decline has been halted and even reversed in some parts of the country. But the size of the worshipping community is still pitifully small compared to that vast 'community' of uncommitted believers. If so many say they believe in God and even claim some degree of adherence to a Church, why do so few actually put in an attendance, and even fewer become active members?

At one level this is the most crucial practical question facing the Christian Church in Britain. All of its other plans—for unity, for social welfare, for inner-city renewal—depend upon the backing of a substantial and committed membership. It is that membership from whom the money, talents and time will come to make all the great plans viable. Without it, the Church is reduced to the level of the worst kind of pressure group: all talk and protest, with no real base in support.

So a great deal of thought has been put into church growth in recent years. Indeed, it is itself a growth industry. Books and conferences have analysed the reasons for decline and offered ways of reversing it: usually techniques based on modern marketing methods. The potential 'market' is analysed. The points of resistance are examined. The means of contact, involvement and finally commitment are taught. It may sound mechanical and vaguely 'secular', but Churches which have employed these methods have often seen quite astonishing growth. I know of a North London suburban church that has seen its regular congregation grow from under 200 to about 700 in five years, with a parallel growth in paid staff (two to nine) and income.

Growth of this kind comes from four sources: biological (by the birth of children in church families), transfer in (people moving to the church from another one, whether locally or far away), transfer across (from fringe to occasional, from occasional to regular churchgoer) and, of course, conversion. Obviously the process can work in reverse. People move away or go to another church. People who were once regular become occasional or sporadic attenders. And people lapse and even apostasise.

My guess is that the decline in churchgoing since the Victorian era is quite simply explained by the second set of examples. More people have left than have joined. People who were once regular churchgoers now attend only occasionally. If that sounds like stating the obvious, it is nevertheless an observation that raises questions about much current evangelistic strategy, which often assumes that the average Briton is totally apathetic about religion, uninformed about the content of the gospel and outside the Church because he rejects its message. I think those assumptions are worth challenging.

Let me start by saying that I accept that large tracts of our great cities are spiritual deserts. Churchgoing in some of them (London's East End, for example) is very low indeed, perhaps as low as 2 per cent. Many of the people who live in these parts are, indeed, apathetic about religion, largely because they seldom meet it in any effective form. Most of the Churches are small and struggling to survive (though often there is a reality and depth of faith among their members that would shame suburbia). Few children go to Sunday school or its equivalent, and knowledge of the content of the Christian faith is hazy and often inaccurate.

But such areas are exceptions. Indeed, that picture is by no means true of all parts of our inner-city areas. Where there is a predominantly Afro-Caribbean population, churches tend to flourish and are demonstrably part of the culture. In Liverpool and parts of West London, where there is a large Roman Catholic population, churchgoing is far higher than that miserable 2 per cent. Unfortunately, various misleading figures have gained credence, especially with the media, and one often hears the assertion that churchgoing is practised by 5 per cent (or sometimes even less) of the population. There is in fact no statistical or evidential basis for such a figure. Over the UK as a whole *weekly* churchgoing is around 14 per cent and occasional churchgoing is nearer 38 per cent.[1]

Thus the urban areas are atypical; it is misleading to base

---

[1] These figures, and those which follow, are from a BBC Broadcasting Research Report, *Aspects of Religious Activities and Beliefs* (1981).

on them an analysis of the attitude of British people to Christianity. Parts of them do indeed represent a mission field, in
the old sense of the term; but with this difference—the
Church is there, in some strength, and with help and support
can provide a base for spiritual renewal. Even in these areas
most people say they believe in God or have a religious
faith, so they are neither pagans nor secularised. Indeed, folk
religion of a kind flourishes, and no group in the population
are more enthusiastic viewers and listeners to the popular end
of religious broadcasting. A smoking flax is not to be
quenched. It would not only be folly but rank arrogance to
treat the inner-city areas as though they were some utterly
unevangelised field.

However, their problems are special. For the rest of the
country, certain fairly well supported generalisations can be
made. Fewer than 20 per cent of the population describe
themselves as 'agnostic, atheist or having no religion'. Some
4 per cent belong to non-Christian religions. The remaining
people are happy to be called 'Christians'. Of those, almost
exactly half never attend a church. More positively, of course,
half do occasionally go to church: and about 20 per cent of
the 'Christians' say they usually attend a service every week,
or most weeks. In this particular survey, just over 17 per cent
claimed to have attended a service within the last seven days.

Now one can read that information in two ways. Negatively, it suggests that such faith as most of these people have
is weak: not strong enough, at any rate, to persuade half of
them to identify themselves publicly with a Church. There
will be no shortage of critics who will say that their claim to be
Christians is totally contradicted by their actions. Christianity
involves confessing Christ, and the very minimum confession,
one might feel, is public identification with his followers. Of
course, there is truth in this, and I am not suggesting that
these hazy 'believers' are fully-fledged disciples, or anything
like it.

But in those gradations of commitment is concealed a more
positive sign. If it is true that 'He who is not with me is
against me' (Mt 12:30), it is also and paradoxically true that
'Whoever is not against you is for you' (Lk 9:50). By the first
test, these non-attending, inactive 'Christians' are disqualified.
By the second, they appear in a more positive light.

However, the BBC Broadcasting Research Survey from which I am quoting—and its genuine neutrality of purpose is its most reassuring attribute—also investigated a far more interesting question: did the present non-churchgoers ever attend church at any time in their past? The answer was 'yes', *60 per cent* had done so at some time, presumably often in childhood. Then were the occasional churchgoers more regular at any time in the past? Again, 'yes': *70 per cent* used to go more often. And finally were those who described themselves as 'frequent churchgoers' even more regular in attendance in the past? Yet again, 'yes': *30 per cent* used to go more often.

There is a pattern here which will be familiar to cinema managers and directors of league football clubs. People still attend these activities, but much less frequently. Churchgoing is not immune to sociological pressures. As the compilers of the BBC report put it:

> The evidence . . . does suggest that whatever may have been the root cause or causes of the decline in churchgoing, its momentum is to be explained in sociological terms. In a previous generation one went to church because 'everybody' went to church and, if for no other reason than the comfort of conformity with the social norm, most people probably enjoyed the experience. But churchgoing is no longer the accepted thing. Not merely does it take no social courage to ask why one should go to church, but the onus is upon those who think we should go to convince us that we should.

We shall return to that 'onus' later. Let us for now look at the reasons why people who once went to church no longer do so. According to the BBC researchers, less than 10 per cent stopped attending 'because they did not believe in Christianity any more'. That in itself is astonishing: it gives a whole new importance to the word 'lapsed'. For comparison, three times as many (30 per cent) stopped attending because they had 'too much to do' and 28 per cent simply because they had 'lost the habit'. A further 15 per cent 'didn't see any point in going to church'. Hardly anybody blamed the clergy or accused Christians of hypocrisy. Churchgoing did not rate as an important enough activity to claim time taken up by gardening, going to the pub, playing sport, visiting relatives and, of course, watching television.

What emerges from this evidence is support for the picture

we have seen emerging throughout this book. Britain has very little anti-clericalism. Few people are *against* the Church or Christianity. Most people, on the contrary, claim to be Christians and say they believe in God. If a mere quarter of them decided that part of that belief was a commitment to regular churchgoing, we would not know where to seat them. A massive church extension programme would have to be launched.

But between that goal and its attainment lie formidable difficulties, both sociological and theological. To the reasons adduced by the BBC report for the decline in churchgoing other observers have added further factors. Many British people feel culturally alienated from the Church: its music, language, style and atmosphere are foreign to their everyday experience. Others find the Church is in general too intellectual. They are lost in a sea of unfamiliar words, expected to sit and listen to closely argued lectures and readings from a book, the Bible, which they often find obscure and baffling. Some, who are otherwise attracted to the Church, are deterred from attending by the fear that once in they will never be able to extricate themselves—'church' will take over their whole lives.

Those are, in general, sociological reasons; and in different ways it may be possible for sensitive church leaders to get round most of them. Many services today are *not* culturally alien—except, perhaps, from the culture of the English public school, the Prayer Book and the *Daily Telegraph*. Not all services or sermons, by any means, are too intellectual. And it is often possible for people to slip into the outer circle of a Church to try the water before deciding to jump right in. What cannot be avoided are the theological reasons for unbelief or half-hearted commitment.

In the end, the Church stands or falls by its message. And that message is an unambiguous one. God exists. He is holy, just and merciful. We have disobeyed his law and are suffering the inevitable consequences of that disobedience now and will suffer them into eternity if we remain as we are. God has sent his Son Jesus to be the Saviour of the world. He died on the cross for our sins. He was raised again to life. Now he offers us forgiveness and new life if we put our trust in him: salvation from the consequences of our rebellion.

It is not a gospel with a lot of 'ifs' or 'buts'. It does not politely request consideration. It demands a response. And every time it confronts us, we make a response to it: for or against. The fundamental Christian confession is 'Jesus is Lord'. That is to say, he has our total allegiance. For that allegiance martyrs gave their lives. In that allegiance the agents of the gospel braved appalling odds to make its message known. Christianity asks a great deal of people, and gives them in return everything that is worth having.

It is that very totality of faith that frightens off the casual, agnostic, would-be believers. They do not want to become fanatics or religious maniacs. They do not want the ordinary pattern of their everyday lives to be turned upside down by an invading conqueror. They do not want to abandon their friends, their hobbies, their pastimes . . . or, I dare say, their sins. They are very interested in the benefits of Christianity. They are aware of an inner need for peace of mind, security and acceptance, and sense that this may in some way be connected with God. But they reject the demands of the gospel. Consequently they come so far—the family service sometimes, Harvest festival, a church wedding—but hold back at the crucial point of commitment.

Now it is very tempting, faced with such a situation, to dilute the demands, and there are probably few of us who have not done it. No great denial of truth is involved. We speak of faith as 'a grain of mustard seed' or—as I have already done—as the 'smoking flax'. We make the distinction David Edwards has made between the occasional attender and 'people like myself who get a lot out of it'.[1] We talk of folk religion—and the basic sense of wonder. The danger is that we are incidentally creating at least two classes of Christians: the 'real' Christians, who believe and pray and go to church and confess Christ in their daily lives; and the 'second-class' Christians (admirable folk, of course) who find all this a bit beyond them but exhibit general good will towards God and the Church and occasionally turn up to swell the congregation on special occasions. What we have done, in effect, is to force a fluid, even dynamic, situation into two distinct categories, not recognising that people move back-

---

[1] In a paper for the Central Religious Advisory Committee, 1986.

wards and forwards between and among these positions, as research shows. Indeed, which 'committed' Christian has never been through a period when their faith could be better described as 'second-class'? And which 'nominal' Christian has never felt the hand of God upon him or her?

The concept of a fringe, an outer circle and an inner circle in church life is a helpful one, but we must not let it become doctrinaire. The object of Christian ministry is to draw *everyone* into the very heart of the Church: nothing less. The observable fact that some hold back, that some are slowly moving inwards and some are sometimes drifting outwards does not alter the fundamental objective: 'attaining to the whole measure of the fullness of Christ . . . we will in all things grow up into him who is the Head' (Eph 4:13–15). We can and should respect folk religion. We can and should cherish and nourish the mustard seed and the smoking flax, but always with the intention that the former will spring into growth and the latter will burst into flame.

It is good news, not bad, that there is in Britain an enormous number of people—well over thirty million—who claim to believe in God, and twenty million who sometimes go to church. They represent the primary area of the Church's ministry. They do not need persuading of the fundamental truth of the Christian case, but they do need to be persuaded that it makes demands as well as bestowing benefits. It is not possible to follow a crucified leader and claim that the path is always painless.

But this ministry must be carried out sensitively. We are *not* calling people to be religious fanatics. We are *not* asking them to abandon their friends, hobbies, sports or even television, provided they are prepared, with God's help, to abandon their sins. We are inviting them to believe in a Lord who can transform, not demolish, the ordinary joys of their daily lives. We are talking of a faith that takes the bits and pieces of life and fashions them into something unbelievably splendid, in which all their friendships, hobbies and interests will be lit up in a totally new way. The Church does not exist to extinguish life, but to offer it 'to the full' (Jn 10:10). It is a major tragedy of our present situation (and largely a heritage of the past) that so many people who feel drawn to God fear that the Church is not the place to pursue that search.

It may be, as David Edwards suggests in the paper already quoted, that 'the British churches will have to settle for something like the present level of attendance'. For myself, I do not think that the proportion of genuinely committed Christians in the population of Britain is any lower now than it was fifty, a hundred, or five hundred years ago. The difference is the degree of active participation by the less committed adherents. If the Churches cannot draw more people from that fringe into their committed membership—as well as winning some of the real 'unbelievers' for the faith—then there seems little prospect of genuine or lasting church growth. The onus, as the BBC report put it, is upon the Churches to demonstrate persuasively why people should move into its inner ranks rather than out of them.

But I believe it can be done, and without diluting the message. Almost every growing church has begun by evangelising its own fringe—but it has also been more successful than the others in holding on to its core members. People who have (as they said) 'lost the habit' of churchgoing will not find it easy to discover it again. It really does involve a change of life-style, or at any rate, of life-pattern. They will need a great deal of support and understanding during the period in which they regain the habit. And they will also have to be persuaded that it is worth it: that belonging to a Church, worshipping God, receiving the sacraments, learning and growing together, is life-enhancing rather than life-limiting. Those who know that to be true are the only ones who can persuade anyone else of its truth.

CHAPTER SIXTEEN

CLOUDS ON THE HORIZON?

I SUPPOSE IT COULD FAIRLY BE ALLEGED THAT THIS BOOK has presented a generally optimistic view of the Church in Britain in the closing decades of the twentieth century. I would not deny that I find many very encouraging signs. Those who were ready to write the Church's obituary twenty years ago have had to stay their pens. The sheer resilience of the Christian faith and of the life of the Christian Church has defied what once looked like an irreversible judgement of history. Christianity has regained self-confidence. It has able leaders. It has massive public support. There seems to me every reason, on the evidence, to suppose that Christianity will not only survive in Britain, but stage a major revival in the next couple of decades.

But that generally optimistic and positive assessment has to be tested not only by the problems and obstacles faced by the Churches now—and they are formidable enough, in all conscience—but by those which appear to lie ahead. In this chapter I want to look at those problems and obstacles—clouds that are on the horizon, or even at present beyond it, but that may well pose formidable hazards for the Churches over the coming generations. Some of the clouds are in fact already overhead, but not all of them have yet become storm clouds. Indeed, some may prove to be bearers of blessings. Some are old problems which may present themselves in a new guise, for all the world like an old disease reappearing in a new and virulent form. A few are completely new, products of scientific advance or philosophical adventure. Taken together, they can be seen as tests of the Church's credibility, for no one will take Christianity seriously if it cannot or will not face challenges of this kind. As Moltmann put it, 'The Church's gospel is the gospel of Jesus Christ, but the Church's context is society'.[1] If the gospel was true nineteen centuries ago, but is irrelevant today, then quite simply it is not 'good news' for this generation. Christianity is an historical religion, but it is one that is always earthed in the *now*.

I should like to look first at the clouds that are coming up within the Church—issues and problems that are found inside the Christian community, even though many of them have their origins in the broader issues of philosophy and sociology. The first (not, I think, in importance, but in timing) concerns ecumenism, in the broadest sense: the idea of the Church as 'one, holy, catholic and apostolic', visibly united in faith and order, as a witness to the world.

THE DILEMMA OF ECUMENISM

The ecumenical movement, as such, has not fared well in Britain in my lifetime, as we have already seen. But now, in the last dozen years of the century, there are undoubtedly new stirrings. The Anglican–Roman Catholic talks (ARCIC) represent one rather formal strand of the debate. Probably more important are the mutterings of rebellion from the ranks. Church people of all denominations, collectively a minority in the community, are becoming less and less patient with the leadership of the Churches. They manage to get along quite well together, for the most part, and cannot see why the legacy of old feuds, disputes and (as they see them) hair-splitting arguments over doctrine should keep them apart.

It is this kind of pressure that gave rise to the Swanwick Conference of church leaders in September 1987. Here there was a genuine note of urgency, fuelled by the results of the 'Not Strangers but Pilgrims' exercise of the previous year. A mood of euphoria seemed to seize many of the delegates

[1] Quoted by John Tiller, *A Strategy for the Church's Ministry* (Church Information Office, 1984).

following a statement by Cardinal Hume that the Roman
Catholic Church would move 'from co-operation to commitment' in the field of unity. 'The most important event in the
field of British Church unity since the Reformation',
announced one church leader: a somewhat excessive reaction,
I would have thought, to a statement which went no further
than (and in some respects fell short of) the Ecumenism document of the Second Vatican Council in the 1960s. Still, I was
not there, and I must accept the word of eminently sensible
people who were that something quite extraordinary
happened at Swanwick. Time will tell how long the flame lit
there will burn and how far its light will shine.

It is all too easy to become cynical about ecumenism, or
even to feel that for all the heady language, nothing has been
achieved, nor will be achieved. In fact, much has changed for
the better, especially at the level of local church activity and
in liaison between church leaders. It is unlikely that we shall
ever return to the situation—as recent as the 1950s—when
Anglicans were as insufferably patronising to Free Church
people as they themselves thought the Roman Catholics were
to Anglicans. After all, until the 1960s Free Church Christians
were technically barred from receiving Communion in the
Church of England: and not only technically, but actually, in
many cases. Now the practice of eucharistic hospitality is
widespread and sanctioned by Canon Law. Non-Catholics are
still generally barred from receiving Communion at Roman
Catholic Masses, though the strict rules are occasionally
waived in practice and occasionally hospitality is officially
permitted in certain well defined cases.

So although little seems to have moved in a formal sense
towards church unity, there have been significant changes of
attitude, which the Inter-Church Process and the Swanwick
Conference probably helped to express, and the 'ecumenical
instrument'—the proposed new structures of inter-church co-
operation—may well symbolise. But if Swanwick is to do
anything to free the log-jam in British ecumenism, it will have
to square some extraordinarily complex circles. For instance,
most of the Free Churches already have women ministers and
the Anglican Churches seem to be moving inexorably in the
same direction. But Rome is unyielding on this issue, and so
is Constantinople. It is much the same with theology. The

Roman Catholic Church under Pope John Paul II has gone a long way towards marginalising liberal and speculative theology. To a lesser degree, the Church of England and the Church of Scotland have also distanced themselves from theological liberalism, while defending its right to existence within the Church. But some of the main Free Churches, at any rate in England and Wales, have continued to allow and teach liberal theology. With the exception of the Baptists, they have been relatively untouched by the swing towards conservative theology. What possible coalition, let alone unity, could be foreseen between the theology of, say, the United Reformed Church and the Vatican?

Not only that, but any Christian unity worth the name must include several substantial and growing areas of Christianity in Britain: the conservative Evangelicals, the Black-led Churches and the charismatic movement. In so far as they are found *within* the main denominations, it is not impossible to imagine parts of these movements surviving and even flourishing in a future united or federal Church. But in their more independent manifestations they are likely to be left out of the argument, which would simply create a new, non-ecumenical grouping outside whatever form the new structure might take. But even the denominational Evangelicals are rather wary of union with Rome, especially if it were to involve recognising the supremacy (in some restated way) of the Pope; and I cannot see the supporters of women's ordination quietly packing up their bags and going away in the interests of some great ecumenical dream Church.

There is the heart of the problem. What vision are we meant to have of this new 'ecumenical instrument?' If it is simply the British Council of Churches reborn, with the Roman Catholic Church as a member, that is hardly the stuff dreams are made of—certainly not 'the greatest step forward since the Reformation'. But if it is more—say, mutual recognition of ministries leading to intercommunion (which *would* be the 'greatest step forward' indeed)—then we are into the minefield of women's ordination, the nature of the eucharist, papal authority and liberal theology. After all, would the Pope *want* to be in communion with the Revd Don Cupitt . . . or even the Bishop of Durham . . . let alone the Revd Ann Pettit?

Like most Anglicans, I am eager to see Church unity. Indeed, I long for the day when I am in communion with my fellow Christians of the Roman obedience, and I am prepared to make a sacrifice of much of our Anglican heritage and swallow a good deal of denominational pride to bring it about. But again, like most Anglicans, I am not prepared to enter into a union which in effect excommunicates many Christians with whom I am now happily in communion. It is, of course, the whole ecumenical dilemma writ large. It will need a hitherto invisible spirit of charity and a largeness of vision to chase away the clouds from the ecumenical scene. Swanwick 1987 may have shed some light, but it will take a larger sun to arise to clear this particular sky.

FUNDAMENTALISM AND SEPARATISM

It is in this context that one must view a number of other internal problems. Biblical fundamentalism, for instance, obstinately refuses to go away. It takes more forms nowadays, and some of it shades away into a kind of respectable conservatism, but real hard-line fundamentalism is also strong, as anyone who has crossed swords with it will discover. It is especially strong in the Reformed camp, in the membership of college and university Christian Unions, in many non-denominational missions and movements and in some publishing houses.

Fundamentalism is well funded, largely by wealthy Christian businessmen, the size of whose bank-balances is sometimes in inverse ratio to the extent of their theological knowledge. It is such people who make the evolution protest movement so effective, for instance, bombarding youth organisations and schools with pseudo-academic literature disproving evolution on biblical grounds. There is, of course, a thoroughly respectable critique to be made of evolutionary philosophy, but this is, for the most part, cranky propaganda masquerading as solid scientific evidence.

The Fundamentalists cannot simply be ignored. They will not go away, nor should they: in many respects they represent a necessary and healthy corrective to the prevalent theological liberalism of the post-war period. Their stress on the primacy of revelation ('God has spoken') and their witness to the reliability and inspiration of the Scriptures is admirable, and shared, of course, by all who take a catholic and orthodox view of truth. The divisive issue is infallibility, when defined as 'verbal inerrancy'. The experience of Anglican evangelicalism in the last twenty years is reassuring in this respect. When the Church as a whole began to take Evangelicals seriously, two remarkable things happened. The Evangelicals stopped trying to defend every tiny bridgehead of doctrine and practice, and began to separate what to them were primary issues from secondary ones. And the Church stopped regarding Evangelicals as a kind of Protestant fifth column in its ranks, giving them the long overdue chance to show what talents, drive and spiritual vision they could bring to its leadership. As a side effect, the fundamentalist issue pretty well disappeared: it is simply not an important question in the Church of England at the present. My guess is that it will only return if Evangelicals are ever again shunted into an ecclesiastical siding, or if the more eccentric kind of liberals are given too great a prominence in the hierarchy or the theological colleges.

Outside the Anglican Churches and the Church of Scotland, however, fundamentalism is alive, well and growing. One must hope that any serious ecumenical dialogue will remember its existence, for Fundamentalists as a group are undoubtedly larger than any one of the English Free Churches.

So, needless to say, are the Charismatics. Again, they do not pose a threat to Christian unity within the historic Churches, but the restoration movement raises a different set of questions. At present relatively small in numbers, it can either hive off to become yet another new denomination on the fringe of traditional Christendom or it may possibly be drawn into a friendly relationship with other evangelical and charismatic groups, including some involved in ecumenical moves. Again, either to ignore or to ostracise these House Churches is a counsel of despair. Many of their leaders, as we have seen, are not obscurantist or separationist by instinct. Perhaps the model of the Ichthus Fellowship in South London—a neo-House Church movement which includes among its affiliated groups one or two Churches also affiliated to the Baptist Union—might be extended to other such movements.

The same could be true of the Black-led Churches. At present, they fall into a multiplicity of groups: many pentecostal, most evangelical in style and language, some Adventist and a few holding various heterodox beliefs about the Trinity, baptism, the spirits of the departed and even occult and animist practices. They have a number of gifted and wise leaders, some of whom are aware of possible dangers ahead, but there are also some who have created idiosyncratic bases for personal advancement and even financial gain. Few White-led Churches have any close relationship with them, and they tend to steer clear of local councils of churches and ministers' fraternals. The West Indian Evangelical Alliance has achieved some success in relating orthodox fellowships to the evangelical mainstream and the British Council of Churches has extended various invitations towards them, but the multiplication of denominations and the growth of urban black ghettoes has nevertheless created an unhealthy religious subculture in many places, completely isolated from other Christian Churches and, indeed, from the rest of society.

The faults by no means all lie on the side of the ethnic Churches. Many of them came into being as a direct consequence of racist attitudes in traditional English congregations. Finding themselves (or feeling themselves to be) unwanted, they formed their own Christian fellowships, with their own leaders and styles of worship. It will be a slow and painful process to repair this breach, or even build effective bridges across it, but a start has been made in places and it must be patiently pursued. Perhaps the experience of an Asian Christian fellowship in North-east London can be a sign of hope. On their own initiative, they approached the local bishop to ask if they could in some way be related to the Church of England. He responded positively; two of their leaders are now preparing for ordination and eventually the whole congregation hopes to be in full communion with the Church of England while retaining their own cultural identity and language in worship.

MALE DOMINATION

The role of women is already a major cloud on the Church sky. Whether it brings a storm or showers of refreshment will depend largely on how it is handled over the next decade or so. It is not simply a matter of the ordination of women to the Anglican priesthood but goes much more deeply into the whole place of women in the Christian community. The feminist revolution which arrived in the West in the seventies and is still going on was never likely to bypass the Church. How could it, when male privilege was more manifestly entrenched there than almost anywhere else except the pavilion at Lord's? Traditionally women have been regarded by the Church as home-builders, child-bearers and -raisers, makers of tea, cleaners of buildings and flower arrangers. The Channel Four soap opera *Brookside* was painfully accurate when it showed a Roman Catholic parish priest responding to a woman parishioner's request to be given 'some task to do for God' by suggesting she took on the choir laundry.

Women *have* advanced in the Church in the last decade, of course: quite spectacularly, in some ways. Women elders, churchwardens and deacons are quite common. Women preach and teach in every denomination. Women distribute the elements at Communion, lead intercessions and read lessons. And there are women—a few—in the higher echelons of most Churches.

But they *are* few. The present trend would have to continue for fifty years at least before women could expect to have any kind of parity with men in the governing bodies of the major non-Roman Catholic denominations. Although there are a number of very able women theologians, theology is still male dominated. Although there are many gifted women preachers, it is hard to think of one who has a national reputation. Feminism, viewed positively, could provide the Church with a rich new source of talent and leadership at a time when it desperately needs it in order to cope with the challenge of the times. But if it is regarded by those at present in leadership as a problem, as an actual or potential menace to be limited or restrained as far as possible, then all that talent will go to waste, and a vast opposition party will build up in the Church, capable of frustrating any hopes of real advance.

Although the question of the role of women in the Church presents itself as a sociological one, it is in fact theological. It is encouraging that a number of theologians, male and female, have tackled it in recent years. The entrenched male privilege of the Church was a product of the dominant cultures in which it developed, including its Jewish origins and its Graeco-Roman nursery, rather than the teaching of Jesus. It is this teaching, with its quite revolutionary emphasis on the dignity of women and their potential in the work of the kingdom,[1] which could provide a theological base for a new approach to the role of women in the Church.

The clouds within the Church, ominous as some of them may look, are for the most part overshadowed by the clouds which arise from the society around and beyond the Church. Many of these clouds are new ones, to which there are few established responses. Scripture and Christian tradition can help us find answers to questions of church unity, biblical interpretation, church order and even the role of women, but when completely new issues arise—sometimes the product of scientific advance—Christians can find few ready guidelines and certainly no simple answers.

A MULTI-FAITH SOCIETY

The presence in Britain of substantial minorities of followers of the world's great non-Christian religions is a case in point. It is a new experience for us. Our theology of 'other faiths' has been forged in a world in which Christianity struggled to survive and compete with paganism and, later, quite successfully carried the gospel to non-Christian lands. When the Church was planted in those places, it was usually as a minority, and again its stance was predetermined. Survival demanded clear-cut distinctives. Compromise would inevitably lead to absorption.

But now the boot is on the other foot. There are probably a million Muslims in Britain, half a million Hindus and 200,000 Sikhs. These are minorities, of course, but substantial ones. They are the product of immigration rather than missionary

[1] See, for instance, Luke 10:38 ff; 23:55–24:11.

work, but their present position is not unlike that of Christians in, say, India or Pakistan. They are surrounded on every side by a dominant culture, in which they wish to live peacefully and pursue their traditional religion. But they cannot ignore the host culture, and the host culture cannot ignore them. A new element, a fresh ingredient is put into the religious pie.

So far the Churches have been unable to settle on a coherent policy towards the other faiths. Many Christians feel that their first responsibility towards them is to share with them the Church's gospel. Others regard that as offensive: they talk about respecting the other faiths, about dialogue with them and even about forming some kind of pan-religious association to foster good relationships and mutual understanding. Probably most simply ignore the presence in Britain of these other faiths—not a difficult thing to do if you live in Powys, Wiltshire or Suffolk. There are, they feel, more pressing problems. Provided that the Muslims and Hindus do not interfere with our religious freedoms or try to enlist our children, they are content to 'live and let live'.

The difficulty is that 'living and letting live' in itself raises important issues. To what extent should the State's educational systems, for instance, institutionalise these distinctions? Are there to be Muslim, Hindu and Sikh schools, as well as Protestant and Catholic ones? Are the other faiths to be given time to broadcast—even a share in the time traditionally given to the Christian Churches? I know for a fact that the appearance of a Muslim or Sikh on *Thought for the Day* on the radio crystallises the problem remarkably for listeners in middle England.

The problem for the Churches is one of attitude. Do they regard the adherents of these other faiths principally as objects of evangelism or as partners, in some sense, in the religious quest? There has been a good deal of sophisticated thinking on this subject,[1] but much of it is necessarily in the realm of theory. Those of us who have had to face the practical implications of it—in education, perhaps, or broadcasting— are aware how different it all looks in the streets of Bradford or Southall when compared with the view from a university department of comparative religion.

---

[1] See, for example, Kenneth Cragg, *The Christ and the Faiths* (SPCK 1986).

For myself, I see no future in either confrontation or compromise. It is frankly impossible in the current state of our society to countenance direct or unfettered competition between the major religions. However much Christians may wish to win Muslims, Hindus or Sikhs for Christ—and I certainly accept that that is a thoroughly desirable objective—it can only be done in a gentle, sensitive, painstaking way, based on genuine respect for the other person's culture and beliefs. The alternative is to create waves of anger, resentment and pain which could blow our fragile communal peace apart. Most Christians have learned this lesson—slowly—where Judaism is concerned. Now we must learn it again with these less accessible religions.

But compromise is also surely no option at all. I remember attending a multi-faith service some years ago, in which Christians, Muslims, Buddhists, Hindus, Sikhs and Jews took part, and vowing never to attend one again. It was not that I felt my faith threatened. Frankly, nobody's faith could be threatened by such a cotton-wool coalition. I felt insulted by the underlying inference that deep down we all believed in the same God, that we were all somehow 'right' and that nobody was to be regarded as 'wrong': and I was pretty sure that any self-respecting Muslim, for instance, would feel exactly the same. To respect another person's deeply held religious beliefs is a sign of maturity and real humanity. But (as I have argued in an earlier chapter) to pretend, in the face of all the facts, that he and I at heart believe the same things is to insult us both and to imply that truth is an adjustable commodity. The 'God' of Buddhism is simply not the God of Abram, Isaac, Joseph and Jesus. Indeed, in the Judaeo-Christian view of things, 'he' is not a 'God' at all, but a concept, an inner reality, not an externally or objectively existing Person at all. What can it possibly mean for a Buddhist and a Christian to 'pray' together? To whom or what on earth or in heaven are they praying? I cannot see inter-faith worship as anything more than a diversion from the real issues, and I know that view is held by many leaders in the other religious communities.

But the Churches must have a coherent policy on this issue, especially where education is concerned. Much religious education, especially in multiracial areas, is syncretistic in content, satisfactory neither to followers of the non-Christian faiths nor to practising Christians. Yet children in modern Britain must be taught how to live peacefully in a multiracial society. Not only that, but there are things we can profitably learn from others whose religious quest begins from different sources and leads along other paths. In that setting—of mutual respect and reverent enquiry—Christians may well be able to share with their neighbours the unique insight into truth which they experience through the Son of God, Jesus.

CHURCH AND STATE

While the Church looks over its shoulder, as it were, at the other faiths, it is also aware that its unique role in British society is threatened by more pressing opposition. Until the post-war era no one seriously challenged the rights of the Christian Church to a major, though mostly unwritten, role in the nation's establishment. Bishops in the House of Lords are only a tiny part of this. The crowning of a new monarch by the Archbishop of Canterbury is nearer the heart of it. So is the assumption that the rector will take the chair at a protest meeting about a new motorway, or the presence in the local paper of a weekly column written by a minister of religion, or the appointment of chaplains to hospitals, the armed forces, shops and factories. The Christian Church has infiltrated every part of our national life, and until recent times no-one has seriously challenged this.

I doubt if it is being challenged now, in any radical way, but I see the possibility of such a challenge as a large cloud just over the horizon. Certainly a government of the extreme left (an unlikely but not impossible scenario) would remove all the Church's positions of privilege, if the experience of some London boroughs is anything to go by. But many would challenge the Church's major influence in education, especially at primary level, and there is a faint but persistent refrain of protest about the protected role (as it is seen) of religious broadcasting on the BBC, ITV and independent local radio. When the Church makes itself unpopular with the government, as it has tended to do in recent years, it is not very surprising that some politicians think in terms of 'teaching it a lesson'—and that could involve a look at the places where the Church has, by tradition, access to the public ear in a unique way.

The Church has, of course, thought a good deal about its relation to the State. The established Churches of England and Scotland like to think of themselves as in some sense guardians of the national conscience, but to fulfil that role they need to hold two conflicting positions in tension. They must not become so identified with the State that criticism sounds like high treason; nor so separated from the State that their protests can be dismissed as merely the product of extremism or sectarianism. They have to be in the society but not of it: a difficult stance to adopt. And the other Churches, which share many of the aspirations of the established ones, need to work out precisely where they stand in this matter, too.

For the voice of the Churches must be heard. The social and scientific revolution of our times rattles on at a breath-taking pace. Someone at some time must cry 'wait'. The family structure of society totters; the number of abortions climbs; the new science of genetic engineering advances; arti-ficial insemination and *in vitro* fertilisation transform the mechanics of what used to be called 'procreation': in a climate like this there must be a coherent, persuasive body of opinion which is inclined to be cautious, which asks awkward and fundamental questions, which challenges the proposition that because a thing *can* be done it *should* be done. Is not the Church, in its broadest sense, just such a body? If it wishes to be a guardian of society's conscience, then it will need to be well informed and courageous, cautious and yet positive. It must do its thinking in the light of biblical teaching and the Christian tradition, and then it must share that thinking with a society that feels itself being dragged along, at times almost out of control, by forces it does not understand. AIDS, and the sexual revolution that was its seed-bed, has made many people think again about the direction in which our society is going, and the speed at which it is getting there.

The difficulty for the Church is the sheer variety of the challenges it faces. People look to it for a lead in such diverse matters as nuclear disarmament, race relations, the regener-ation of the inner city, sexual morality, medical ethics, crime and punishment, health and healing and even the care of the dying. Once, when the Church was virtually synonymous with the nation, it was not unreasonable to ask of it a polymathic competence in the realms of science, art, politics and morality. But now the Church's resources, both human and financial, are less, while the demands are even greater. Yet every one of the issues put to it carries within it the seeds of blessing or of destruction, so that the Church cannot say—as some politicians and newspaper editors would like it to—that it is not a proper area of Christian concern. The gospel is a message of human and social transformation whose effects cannot be limited to what we may narrowly call the 'religious' realm. While men and women find their humanity denied by the conditions in which they live; while the whole concept of the family is under siege; while our prisons are overcrowded and our schools doctrinal battlegrounds, the Church of the incarnate Son of God cannot stand idly by.

It is hard to say which of all these issues will most occupy the Church's attention over the next decade. One hopes that it will not be some matter of internal religious politics, like further liturgical reform, the ordination of women to the priesthood, or church unity. It may be a slightly more 'open' but specifically religious topic—perhaps the orthodox–liberal argument will burst into flame again, possibly over the issue of the miraculous. The renewal of the inner cities will undoubtedly be high on the agenda and may well be joined by a similar concern for the depopulated and largely unchurched countryside.

My own guess is that issues of sexual morality will continue to be at the top of the agenda: not by the Church's choice, but by public demand. The gay liberation movement, thrown into some disarray in 1987 by government moves to curb the teaching of homosexual ideas in schools and the Church of England's firm rejection of homosexual practice, will surely return to the fray, perhaps when AIDS is on the wane. Divorce (and remarriage in church) will continue to trouble religious people. It may well be that a major issue to be faced before the turn of the century will be the new omniscience of the computer and so-called artificial intelligence. Are there limits to the extent to which electronic machinery can organise and run our lives? And, if so, what are they?

All of these things—every one of these looming clouds—challenge the credibility of the Church and its gospel. Perhaps the time is ripe for a genuine reversal of thinking, even on the part of Christians. As Bishop Lesslie Newbigin has pointed out, we have become accustomed to viewing Christianity through the eyes of our culture: and perhaps I have at times been guilty of that in this book. That is to make 'our culture'—our presuppositions and perspectives—the determining factor, rather than the gospel itself. Perhaps the time has come for us to reverse that process, and look again at our culture through the eyes of Christianity.

It may not be a pretty sight, but it may be the first and essential step towards putting it right.

CHAPTER SEVENTEEN

THE PRIORITY OF THE SPIRIT

SOME YEARS AGO THERE WAS A SENIOR FIGURE AT THE BBC who liked to put the religious broad-casters in their place. To him, they were all closet lefties or frustrated political journalists, desperate to be 'relevant' and 'worldlier than thou'.

'Why', he would roar across his office, 'Why can't you just stick to *proper religion*?'

By 'proper' religion, one soon learned, he meant saying prayers, singing hymns and talking about God. He certainly did *not* regard the plight of the impoverished elderly as a proper subject of religious concern, despite St James' quite categorical statement that 50 per cent of 'pure and faultless religion' is looking after 'widows and orphans in their distress' (Jas 1:27). His views are frequently echoed in the newspapers and politicians' speeches: the bishops and clergy should talk more about God.

Oddly enough, they have been doing so for many years, but it takes a long while for changes inside the Church to filter through to non-churchgoers, especially to those with closed minds. There has been an enormous revival of interest in what we might call the spiritual dimension of Christianity in the last decade. It is the most common topic of religious books. It is the constant theme of conferences, retreats and workshops. I do not believe the churches ever banished God from their thinking, but if there were any truth in the idea that worldly concerns had become dominant in the Church, it ceased to be so many years ago.

I did not want to end this book with a chapter on problems, or church politics, or Christian strategy. The most fitting final chapter, for me, is one that asks about the spiritual life of the modern Church: if you like, that takes its spiritual temperature. Is it a praying Church? Is it a Church that knows where its inner resources are to be found? Does it truly believe in God and does it experience the life of the Spirit? A Church that outwardly prospers but is dead within cannot expect to survive ridicule or criticism, let alone downright persecution. But a Church that knows how to confide in God has an inner assurance that outward circumstances simply cannot touch. In other words, the most important question, which I have deliberately left to the very end, is this: how is the *soul* of the Church in Britain today?

In fact, 'soul' is a word not often used in modern Christianity: indeed, hardly heard at all except in hymns. And that is for good theological reasons. In biblical terms, a human being is body, mind and spirit. The lower nature, the 'flesh', consists of body and mind. So when people talk of 'saving their soul' (in the sense of 'getting to heaven') they really mean 'saving their spirit'. It is in that sense that I ask how is the soul of the Church: I mean its 'spirit', that part of its life that relates directly to God.

Christianity as a religion addresses itself to all three parts of human nature: to body, mind and spirit. To the body it speaks of an incarnate Son of God, one with us in experience of mortality, concerned that our eating, drinking, working, lovemaking, singing and dancing should be sanctified. To the mind it speaks of truth incarnate, of wisdom revealed and proclaimed, a faith in an infinite personal God that makes universal sense of all the minute particulars of our imperfect human knowledge. And to the spirit it speaks of union with God, of knowing him and enjoying him for ever.

All these elements should be in perfect balance, but of course they seldom are. Often the Church has been so intent on finding union with the divine that it has despised the God-given material world. Often it has been so obsessed with the minutiae of doctrine, with meticulous definition of truth, that it has blinded itself to the person who called himself 'the truth'. And often it has so concerned itself with the affairs of this world that it has completely lost sight of the eternal one.

I think it is true that there was a time in the post-war decades, perhaps most noticeably in the 1960s, when a good deal of British Christianity became somewhat secularised, but that was partly at least a reaction against a kind of pietism that preached the salvation of 'souls' (as it called them) rather than whole persons and regarded any concern about wider issues of justice and righteousness as a 'social gospel'.

As I have said, I think that era has passed, partly because more and more Christians have seen that *both* positions are wrong if held exclusively, and partly because human beings, made in God's image, are hungry above all for him. No solution to their real needs can be satisfactory if it ignores that elementary truth about human nature: 'You have made us for yourself', as Augustine wrote, 'and our hearts are restless until they find their rest in you.' No gospel is truly of God if it ignores injustice, greed, exploitation and suffering. But no gospel is truly good news if it does not also meet the deepest hunger of the human heart, and that is a hunger for God.

HUNGER FOR GOD

Unquestionably that hunger is more recognised in the Church today than it was twenty years ago. I can see evidence for that hunger in the response we receive to religious broadcasts. The most instant and intense response is evoked by broadcasters who address themselves to those fundamental longings of the human spirit. Prayer, meditation, contemplation, the inner life, space and silence: those are the subjects about which many modern people want to hear, if only because they stand in stark contrast to the world we have created and which surrounds us—a world of demand, controversy, anxiety, image, tension and pressure. A young business woman I know chose to spend the Christmas of 1987 in a convent. She came back to her work a new woman. Space, silence, calm, acceptance, worship: these had renewed her in a way parties and over-indulgence could never do.

Indeed, retreat houses have never been more flourishing. There are literally hundreds of retreat houses all over the country, and many of them are never empty. It is as though the modern world has stumbled across the antidote to its self-created poison. Of course, a retreat can be dismissed as mere self-indulgence—literally a 'retreat' from the stern battle of life, a kind of cowardly withdrawal from the real world. But in truth it is more like an interval in a battle, a pause for breath in an endless struggle for survival. It is not really self-indulgent to draw aside—as Jesus himself did (Mk 1:35)—to renew our spirits and our vision before inevitably launching ourselves back into the bruising world of today. One of the most influential of these retreat houses, Lee Abbey, has always had the aim of sending its guests back into society recharged for mission.

People are turning to retreat houses because it is increasingly difficult to find the space or silence necessary if we are occasionally to hear the voice of God. That is their chief contribution: an environment in which the believer can 'be still and know that I am God'. Even church life today is hectic, especially for the committed church members. There is a kind of spiritual burn-out that can afflict those who for the highest of motives spend all their spare time in church activities, running this, organising that, sitting on committees, leading house groups, sharing in pastoral visiting. Such people need the space and silence of a retreat house every bit as much as the exhausted executive, the desperate young mother or the frantic salesman.

Just occasionally Christians need to be told that it is all right for them to think mainly about themselves. That is one of the strengths of a retreat. For once, we can forget those spiritual responsibilities that weigh so heavily on us, or those family or work burdens, and focus our attention on our own inner needs. It would be self-indulgent if it became a way of life, but for a few days it is as necessary as honestly describing our symptoms to a doctor when we are unwell. There is a way of healing, but it involves opening up the wound. There is a peace that God alone can give, but it comes after we have faced the waves. The routine of prayer, worship, Eucharist, silence, meditation—together, for many people, with confession (the sacrament of reconciliation)—has a way of bringing us closer and closer to the God we believe in but so often try to keep at a distance.

HUNGER FOR PRAYER

The last decade has also seen much renewed emphasis on prayer. Part of that is due to a heated theological debate about the nature and purpose of prayer. Is it, as Christians have traditionally assumed, a means of *involving* God in an active way in our predicament (what David Jenkins calls invoking a 'laser-beam' God)? Or is it an exercise in *submission*, a recognition of the presence of God in everything and every situation, without any expectation that he would actually do anything about changing it? I suppose most Christians, of both schools of thought (which are not entirely mutually exclusive), would agree that prayer is not primarily 'getting God to do what I want' but 'asking God to make me want what he wants'. But most Christians, again, would not feel that this excluded God from *acting* to change things as well as me. It is hard to believe in the God of the Passover and the Red Sea, or the God of the Incarnation and Resurrection, and not to believe that he is able to act, and act decisively, on behalf of his people.

However, quite aside from the theological arguments, there has been a renewed interest in prayer itself. Twenty years ago it was rare to find any Church other than an obviously evangelical one where people prayed spontaneously together. Now it is quite commonplace in Churches of all traditions. Prayer cells and groups in people's homes have helped to deliver British Christians from the inhibitions that kept them from ever praying aloud or expressing their deepest longings before other people. Some people have found further release through the practice of praying in tongues. Others have come to value the great treasure store of devotion in various liturgies, psalters and collections of prayers. Yet others, after half a lifetime of incessantly nagging God, have discovered with a sigh of relief the liberation of praying in silence. And of course many people have found all four. Any Church that advertises a course on the subject of prayer will find a ready response, just as books on the subject invariably sell well. The great age of electronic garbage has also become the great age of prayer.

HUNGER FOR THE WORD

Ours has also become in many ways the new age of the Bible. I can remember a time, twenty or thirty years ago, when it seemed a serious possibility that modern scholarship might effectively marginalise the Bible in the life of the mainstream Churches. I am thinking of the era of de-mythologising, when some scholars were so busy stripping off layer upon layer of 'myth' that one feared literally nothing would be left. In fact, as so often, the Bible proved its own best defence. Karl Barth helped many to see the Scriptures in a more dynamic way as the word of God, and a whole new generation of biblical scholars emerged who treated the Bible with reverence, though not superstition.

Yet the real change, if we are considering the Church's spiritual health, was not in the views scholars held of the Bible but in the use ordinary Christians made of it. New translations, new Bible handbooks and popular commentaries, radio and television programmes and a fresh emphasis on biblical preaching all helped. So, in the Roman Catholic Church, did the new emphasis on *personal* Bible reading, in the home and in small groups. But, most of all, the change was simply in the way Christians came to regard the Bible— and not just the Evangelicals. It is significant that the Liberation Theology movement, by far the most radical expression of Christianity to make an impact on the modern Church, is deeply, almost literalistically, biblical. One may not always, or often, agree with its interpretation, but it was born out of basic communities who actually studied the Bible together, and its chief motivation is the recorded teaching of Jesus in the gospels.

The charismatic movement, too, feeds on a dynamic use of the Scriptures, far removed from the cool exposition so beloved of classical Evangelicals. Indeed, it is nearer the allegorical style of the early Church Fathers. Again, one does not have to agree with it to see that this has created in enormous numbers of Christians not only a deep respect for the Bible but a real hunger for it. The Bible 'comes alive' when it is not only read and studied, but put to use. As St James says, 'Do not merely listen to the word . . . Do what it says' (Jas 1:22).

But the new interest in the Bible does not stop with groups like the Charismatics and the Liberation Theology movement. It is to be found throughout the Church and across the denominations. Just as prayer has been released from the chancel stall, so the Bible has been liberated from the lectern and given back to the people. It has to be said, for instance, that David Jenkins, whose views on the Virgin Birth and the empty tomb scandalised many Christians in 1986, has a remarkable ability to stimulate interest in the Bible as a living vehicle of divine communication. Again, one does not have to agree with his views to recognise the fact that huge crowds turn out to hear him, and often go home from his meetings to blow the dust off their Bibles and start reading them again.

The essential element in this scriptural renewal, I believe, is a recognition—much more widespread now than it was a couple of decades ago—that the Bible is divinely inspired. This is not necessarily the same thing as believing it to be verbally inerrant, of course, but it is a great deal more than saying that it merely 'contains' the word of God. Much modern spirituality springs directly from the idea that the Bible is a dynamic word, a 'sword of the Spirit', a sacramental word conveying grace.

I remember a middle-aged woman being interviewed on a *Songs of Praise* programme from Bangor, in North Wales.[1] She was the mother of a blind physically and mentally handicapped son, a 'cradle Catholic', as she described herself. She radiated faith. Indeed, she said that her son had revealed the love of God in their family: he was himself a 'gospel'—good news of God's love and strength for those who needed it. Her choice of hymn was a paraphrase of a verse in Jeremiah: 'O the word of my Lord', and her reason for choosing it was simple: 'If it were not for the word of God hidden in my heart, in the centre of my life, I could not have survived.' That is what I mean by the Bible as a dynamic spiritual force, a word conveying grace. In the modern church it is being daily experienced by Christians in many different ways, and understood or explained in many different ways. But it is the same word, 'God-breathed', as St Paul calls it (1 Tim 3:16),

---

[1] 10 January 1988.

that is at work, whether in an Ignatian spiritual exercise, a charismatic prayer group or an evangelical 'cell'.

HUNGER FOR THE EUCHARIST

The third element in this renewal of spirituality is, I believe, a fresh appreciation of the Eucharist. There has been a widespread rediscovery of its centrality in much Protestant church life, while the Catholics, as we have seen, have moved from a largely priest-centred understanding of the Eucharist to a people-centred one: an expression of the priestly role of the whole people of God.

Derek Worlock, Roman Catholic Archbishop of Liverpool, has related how the Second Vatican Council originally intended to start its consideration of the Church with the liturgy, but that in the preparation stages it became clear that it must begin with the idea of the 'people of God': 'a people holding different ministries and tasks, but with shared dignity and responsibility for the mission entrusted by Christ to his followers.'[1] This is the insight that transforms the Council's teaching on the Eucharist. That same change of emphasis has led many churches in the Reformed and evangelical traditions to rethink their understanding of Communion. In my youth it was an 'extra' service for the specially holy, or the specially old, usually held at 8 am on a Sunday, or tacked on after a 'word-centred' service. Today, in all kinds of Churches—and not least charismatic ones—Christians have discovered that this service, more than any other, not only celebrates and affirms their unity and fellowship in Christ, but is also a means by which he comes to them in new ways.

I was on the panel of judges which gave the Collins Book Award for 1987 to Father Gerard Hughes for his book of spiritual guidance, *God of Surprises*. What led us to choose it was its total commitment—on the part of a man who was deeply involved (and had been all his life) in issues of peace and justice—to the priority of the inner life:

> The real battle is not in working to change the structure of the Church and of society, but in struggling to change the structure of

[1] Derek Worlock, *Better Together* (Hodder, 1988), pp. 13, 14.

my own psyche. This may sound very individualistic and selfish, but the only thing we can change is ourselves, for the only power that can bring creative change is God . . . all I can do is let his glory through in me, let God be God in my life.[1]

But for Gerard Hughes an essential part of that process is a renewed and demystified understanding of the Eucharist. Our vision of it has been too limited.

> We turn this symbol of the reality of God's love for all his creatures into a sacred object, a thing, and we do not allow God to be God to us even in this most simple and wonderful sign. . . . The Eucharist is given to us so that Christ's presence may be real in the lives of his people, a presence living in our attitudes and values, in our thinking, speaking and style of living.[2]

It is this idea of the Eucharist, the 'breaking of bread', as celebrating and affirming the presence of Christ among his people, and themselves therefore as truly the body of Christ, that has made all the difference. An obsession with privacy, or ritual, or validity, seems to contradict the whole direction of the ordinance. It was given to us for our good, our collective as well as our individual good. As such, it is an essential part of the healthy and balanced Christian life, bringing together in one action man as body, mind and spirit and God as Creator, redeemer and presence.

Prayer, Bible and Eucharist are certainly the heart of the spiritual life of the Church today, as indeed they have been since apostolic times. But prayer can become formal, routine or mechanical. The Bible can be treated as an almanac of religious knowledge. The Eucharist (in Gerard Hughes' phrase) can be regarded as a 'thing', a sacred object rather than as a living symbol of Christ's presence. As in many areas of religious life, from time to time even our most holy practices need to be re-examined if the spiritual life of the Church is to be truly healthy. And this process, of renewal and reformation, has to be continuous, because the process of secularising the sacred is also continuous. The battle is never finally won this side of heaven; but that means that it is also never finally lost.

The Churches of Britain today are caught up in this process of renewal more evidently than at any previous time during

---

[1] Gerard Hughes, *God of Surprises* (Darton, Longman & Todd, 1985), p. 154.
[2] Gerard Hughes, *op cit* p. 132.

my life. It is hard to say whether people are praying more, or reading the Bible more eagerly, or breaking bread together with greater meaning and purpose. However, it is possible to say that all the outward signs suggest a distinct rise in the spiritual temperature, and that this appears to be common more or less across the whole spectrum of church life.

If this is so, and if the rise continues, that may well prove to be the single most important and influential fact recorded in this book, far more significant than statistics of membership or ministry. Every New Testament metaphor of the Church—bride, body, vine—requires life to flow through its members: the life of Christ himself. Without that, it is an empty shrine. But given that divine life, the 'living water' that flows from the throne of God and of the Lamb (Rev 22:1), there is nothing that the Church of Christ cannot achieve. Before that life the gates of the grave fly open. By that life the nations are healed. In that life the old order of things passes away, and everything is made new.

BIBLIOGRAPHY

Edwards, David L. *Christian England, Vol III*. Collins, 1984.
—. *The Futures of Christianity*. Hodder & Stoughton, 1987.
Hastings, Adrian. *A History of English Christianity 1920–1985*. Collins 1986.
Newbigin, Lesslie. *The Other Side of 84*. British Council of Churches, 1983.
Penhale, Francis. *Catholics in Crisis*. Mowbray 1986.
Reid, Gavin. *To Reach a Nation*. Hodder & Stoughton, 1987.
Saward, Michael. *Evangelicals on the Move*. Mowbray 1987.
Walker, Andrew. *Restoring the Kingdom*. Hodder & Stoughton, 1985.
Whale, John. *The Future of Anglicanism*. Mowbray, 1988.

INDEX

Wesley, John 24–25, 78, 104–5, 107, 124
West Indian Evangelical Alliance 196
Westminster Abbey 51
Westminster, Archbishop of 94, 98, 192
Westminster Chapel 57, 115
Westminster Fellowship 57, 117
Westwood, Bill 83
Whitby, Abbey of 19
Whitby, Synod of (664) 19
White, Margaret 165
Whitefield, George 24, 105
Widesfrid, St 98
Wigglesworth, Smith 124
William I 19
Wilson, Des 151
Wilson, Harold 113
Wimber, John 129
Winward, Stephen 114

Women, ordination of 31, 80, 81, 82, 85, 93, 96, 101, 145, 192, 193, 197–98, 203
Wood, Maurice 56
Wood, Wilfred 155
Woolwich 34
World Council of Churches 92
World War I 12, 53
World War II 12–13, 52–53, 54
Worlock, Derek 99, 212
Worship 28–29, 32, 41–52, 61, 81, 93, 110–11, 130, 138–39, 208–9; *see also* Communion, Liturgy, Mass
Wycliffe, John 20–21

YMCA 151
York 84; Archbishop of 77, 82; Dean of 53
York Minster 77